BURNOUT

BURNOUT

What Happens When
Stress Gets Out of Control
and How to Regain Your Sanity

Ken Powell

BA, MSc, AFBPsS C Psychol

"I prescribe this book"
Dr Mike Smith

Thorsons
An Imprint of HarperCollins*Publishers*

Thorsons
An Imprint of HarperCollins*Publishers*
77–85 Fulham Palace Road,
Hammersmith, London W6 8JB
Published by Thorsons 1993

1 3 5 7 9 10 8 6 4 2

© Ken Powell 1993

Ken Powell asserts the moral right to
be identified as the author of this work

A catalogue record for this book
is available from the British Library

ISBN 0 7225 2649 0

Typeset by Harper Phototypesetters Limited,
Northampton, England
Printed in Great Britain by
HarperCollinsManufacturing Glasgow

CONTENTS

ACKNOWLEDGEMENTS

A special thank you is due to all those who provided material for this book from their own experiences of burnout. Some were clients, others agreed to personal interviews, others wrote down their stories. As far as possible they are told in their own words with only a few alterations to ensure anonymity.

Thanks also to Barabara, my wife, for patiently typing and retyping this book.

PREFACE

Burnout, an intense form of stress, affects many people. It leaves sufferers feeling devoid of energy, unproductive and cut off from others. Those in the caring professions – social workers, nurses, doctors and teachers – often experience daily stress because of the nature of their jobs. But they are not the only ones: those who care for elderly and infirm relatives at home, mothers, housewives, business executives, small-business owners, students, people in the armed forces, the disabled and those trapped in unsatisfactory relationships can all know what it's like to face each day full of tension and dread.

This book aims to help you find a way out of your burnout or stress – even though you may feel at present that this is impossible. It provides suggestions for immediate first aid. It then looks at wider issues – at the personal meaning hidden behind stressful events in your life. It will show how these meanings can be changed – in more positive and constructive ways. It provides techniques to increase your personal effectiveness: how to be more assertive, how to manage time, how to relax so that you reduce the harmful physiological and psychological effects of stress.

Teachers, social workers, businesspeople and others in demanding professions have contributed to this book, describing their condition and circumstances and what helped them. Additionally, many others who have been helped to work through their problems in group and one-to-one sessions have provided their insights into ways out of even the most severe cases of burnout.

1

THE WORLD OF BURNOUT

Burnout is a state of mental exhaustion and emotional drain. It results from continually striving to meet the demands of living – despite weeks, months or even years of ongoing stress, frequently intensified by one particularly stressful event.

This one additional event – dramatic or trivial – tips the balance. Burnout is the final response to cumulative, long-term negative stress. It especially affects those who have continued to accept the obligations of their responsibilities despite inadequate resources and not knowing where they stand or what is really expected of them. Burnout is a reaction to the last of a progression of unsuccessful attempts to cope with a variety of negative stressful events.

Burnout leaves us mentally and physically exhausted, feeling cut off from people and achieving little despite squeezing the last drops of our remaining energy.

Burnout leaves us going home with nothing left to contribute to family life. We feel helpless, hopeless, stuck in a tunnel with no end in sight. We see ourselves as useless. We find it difficult to relate constructively to others – fellow employees, clients, students or customers. We have lost all emotion and can only treat others in a detached and dehumanizing way. We may act in an authoritarian manner –

just demanding that others do what we say. This how we try to cope.

Burnout is the price of achievement. It is the price paid by the conscientious who keep going despite their private hells. If this applies to you, you try to carry on, with decreasing effectiveness, attempting to compensate by dragging even more energy from your rapidly depleting stock.

You may try to alleviate your problems in non-productive ways: drinking too much; overeating (usually over-rich, unhealthy foods); smoking heavily; relying on anti-depressants or tranquillizers; ignoring and failing to face difficult issues; procrastinating as long as possible.

You are depressed and anxious, with an ever-present undercurrent of irritability. You feel resentful, unco-operative, defensive, alienated and sometimes immobilized – going through the motions of what you are supposed to do.

Still you force yourself to cope. This is your problem. You are one of the heroes of modern society. You, at least, try to do what you must. Those especially affected are teachers, social workers, counsellors, police officers and doctors. So are many mothers attempting to bring up children with insufficient resources, and executives whose prime aim in life is to meet the demands of the corporation – whatever the cost.

This book is about finding your own personal way out of burnout. It is about getting control over your life, moving forward, releasing your energies and potential. It is for those who are stuck and don't know what to do. It is for those who have opted out, who feel helpless and powerless.

This book is also for those who are at the edge of burnout and who, vaguely or clearly, see what is likely to happen unless they start to take effective control of their lives – and soon.

Tom is a stocky, tense person with a nervous energy he invests in just about everything he does. His fingers tap agitatedly as he talks. The lines on his face intensify what he says.

Tom has worked in the marketing department of a large organization for just over 15 years. He is successful. He has to be – 'Type A' personalities are like that. They have an inner drive to get things done. They talk rapidly. They move fast. Business organizations value and reinforce such behaviour. It energizes their plans.

Tom is thinking of killing himself. If you'd known Tom a few years ago, you'd have thought he could tackle anything.

Tom's troubles started about five years ago. To begin with, things seemed much the same as they'd always been. Tom's firm started to examine ways in which it could become more productive. Staffing levels were cut. Quality was to be enhanced and employees pushed to achieve more 'in the new realism of today's tough economic climate'. Tom gladly accepted the new demands. He pushed himself and his staff harder. At six or seven in the evening, Tom would stuff his briefcase with unfinished business and drive himself the 18 miles home.

He drove his car as he drove himself – fast and ruthlessly. His biggest frustration was slow drivers. Tom felt they could not appreciate the value of time.

His children got used to a father who was physically at home but really out of bounds to them most evenings. Janette, Tom's wife, began to develop other interests. She resumed her studies, obtained a job and began to find life more fulfilling than ever before. The few times Tom wanted to be with his wife, she was busy with her own interests. Rows developed, and eventually Janette saw no point in being married to Tom. He impeded her new life. They were divorced. Tom was shattered.

His response was to throw himself even more into his work. But his performance began to suffer. Errors of judgement and detail began to increase. He saw himself not meeting his own high standards. He used the only technique he knew for dealing with the problem – he put even more effort into what he was doing. He developed tunnel vision: he could only deal with one thing at a time. He was unaware of other issues. He could not think out the wider consequences of his actions. He needed to get the next pressing task done first. All his energy went into it. His next mistake was a major one. He received an official warning. His bonus was cut. His performance rating slumped from 'above average' to 'below average'. He started to argue with colleagues. He became more aggressive. He gradually lost the support of his staff.

Tom's manager gave him three months to pull himself together. Tom now felt he was on a financial tightrope. He had to contribute to his children's well-being, pay part of the mortgage on the home his ex-wife and children lived in and cover the cost of his own flat. When his bonus was cut, his outgoings exceeded his income. He sank into debt. He borrowed more. He 'forgot' to pay bills. Next thing he knew he was summoned to appear in court because he had not responded to an important demand.

Tom did not kill himself, but his progress to a new life wasn't easy.

Analysing Tom's problem isn't easy, either. There were many contributing factors. Tom needed a life that was stressful. This is how he got things done. He learned to cope. He managed, despite his stress, to appear to stay on top of his demanding job. Each additional misfortune added to his burden. The immediate 'cause' of his breakdown was the impending court case. But this is misleading. It was the last straw, the final factor that pushed Tom over the edge.

Stress is like this. You learn to cope, but unless you learn to take positive action to deal with what you perceive as stressful, there usually (but not always) comes a day when one additional factor (perhaps insignificant itself) is too much.

We all differ. Not all burnout is caused by a series of unfortunate events, as was Tom's. But there is a pattern to burnout:

Stressful events enter all our lives → We attempt to cope → An additional factor makes it all too much → The resources within ourselves and provided to us are inadequate to meet the needs of what we have to do.

At the latter stage of burnout we are shouting to ourselves: 'STOP.' But we continue to push. And as we fail to listen, our body takes over and forces us to cease, frequently through illness.

Of course, stress can be a positive thing. Without it there is little drive, motivation or challenge. As pressures increase so does our performance. We enjoy the demands made on us. But too much stress is harmful. Our capacity to perform declines until it reaches a point where we can hardly perform at all. The following graph illustrates how this works.

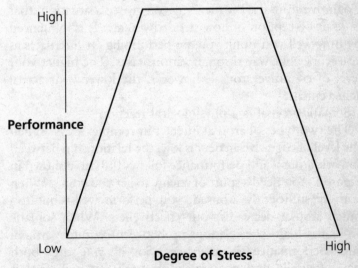

Figure 1: Stress and Performance/1

We all need some tension. Actors, musicians, public speakers and others need an inner tension to perform – so do the rest of us.

If we live under continuous pressure, our body adapts. We learn to cope. Maybe we manage for a few weeks, months or even years, but then some additional burden is placed on us and we find we can cope no longer. The cumulative effects of stress gradually overwhelm our defences.

Figure 1 is perhaps too simplistic an illustration of the complex way stress affects our lives. The 'degree of stress' line (arousal) may consist of two, not one, entities – only partly related:

- cognitive stress, also known as cognitive arousal or cognitive anxiety, and
- somatic stress, or somatic arousal.

Cognitive arousal is the meaning you give to a situation; that is, your perception of how stressed you are. It is influenced by how well you think you are performing. It fluctuates as you work your way through various tasks. The higher your level of cognitive arousal, however, the lower your actual achievement.

Somatic arousal is a physiological reaction.

The two types of arousal interact in complex ways. When the level of cognitive anxiety is low, the relationship between somatic arousal and performance follows the curve shown in Figure 1. You need a spurt of energy to get you going. When you are sufficiently aroused, you perform well – but too much arousal decreases your effectiveness. When somatic arousal is high, the relationship between cognitive arousal and performance is negative. So if you are both physiologically and cognitively aroused, you will find it difficult to produce good results: the more anxious you are, the less well you perform.

The change-over from good performance to poor performance may not be gradual, as Figure 2 shows:

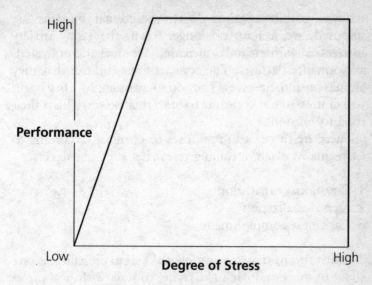

Figure 2: Stress and Performance/2

The extra increment of arousal does not produce a small, gradual change but a dramatic, sudden – and negative – one. So when you try to cut things down, it doesn't work. You are over the top.

There are two more pieces to the puzzle: first, the complexity of your task is related to performance. Difficult goals are challenging, they are motivating and they increase performance – but only if you have willingly accepted the challenge. Challenge that is forced on you is harmful, not exciting. Two persons of equal ability and with similar tasks perform differently if one 'owns' the task and the other has been forced to do it. You can observe this in real life by considering nurses. Many start their careers full of idealism. At this point they 'own' their task. They are willing to overcome difficulties because they accept the goals they have set themselves.

The other factor which complicates the issue is that anxiety reduces goal acceptance. When additional burdens are imposed, we feel we no longer 'own' the task. Anxiety intensifies as demands increase. We feel demotivated. Performance declines. The conscientious still feel that they should push themselves. They do so unwillingly. They begin to feel stressed but continue to force themselves. This is their road to burnout.

There are three main responses to burnout, according to Christina Maslach, a leading researcher on the subject:

1. Emotional exhaustion
2. Depersonalization
3. Lack of accomplishment

The first means that even simple tasks seem difficult. As one client of mine said: 'It's like trying to walk with heavy lead weights attached to each shoe. Each step is difficult and thinking of the whole walk makes it seem impossible.'

Depersonalization is the word used to describe how we distance ourselves from others. As one nurse said; 'I give care like an automatic, wind-up toy. I'm still attending to safety and accuracy, but I feel empty and far away. Nothing touches me any more.' The cumulative effects of stress gradually overwhelm our defences, forcing physical withdrawal. We may not even care for ourselves.

Our problems become compounded. We lose important social networks: friends, partners and colleagues with whom we could share our problems. And sharing such problems is healthy and helps us cope better.

Many in the caring professions suffer burnout because although they originally wanted to do something valuable with their lives, they find that the demands have become too great. Their sense of mission is replaced by a loss of spirit and resignation.

Burnout has qualities similar to depression. Those who are

'obsessive-compulsive' – that is, over-identify with the patients in their care – are more likely to suffer from burnout, as are perfectionists who find it difficult to forgive themselves for failing to meet their own high standards. Perfectionists, because of their nature, find it difficult to make decisions when faced with complex problems. They weigh up the pros and cons again and again. And when they have finally made up their minds, they begin to realize the defects of their decision and their doubts start all over again.

Others who suffer burnout include those who are over-reliant on other people, who need to be directed in what they have to do and to receive frequent reassurance that others approve of them.

So there are many factors linked to burnout: our personality traits – including hostility, obsessive-compulsive behaviour, overdependency and low self-esteem. Circumstances, too, play their part. These can include work overload, unfair treatment and a lack of clarity about what is expected of us.

References

C. Cherniss, *Staff Burnout* (Sage, 1980).

H. Firth et al., 'Professional depression, burnout and the personality in longstay nursing', *Institute of Nursing Studies*, 24.3, 1987.

L. Hardy and L. Parfitt, 'A catastrophe model of anxiety and performance', *British Journal of Psychology*, 82, 1991.

Christina Maslach, 'Burned out', *Human Behaviour*, 5, 1976.

——, *Burnout: The Cost of Caring* (Prentice-Hall, 1981).

A. M. Pines et al., *Burnout: from Tedium to Personal Growth* (Free Press, 1981.)

H. Seyle, *Stress without Distress* (J.B. Lippincott, 1974.)

C.L. Thompson, 'Stress related to nursing', unpublished assignment, 1991.

2

BURNOUT
FROM WITHIN

The stories in this chapter will demonstrate the complex nature of burnout. Some are tales of healthy people becoming contaminated by sick organizations. Others describe the interaction between an organization and the individual. For a few, personality traits played the biggest part in their burnout; but for many it was their work itself that was the major contributor. Working with disabled people, the underprivileged and the terminally ill requires a special sort of sensitivity – and sensitive people break more easily.

Figure 3 shows one way of summing up burnout.

Yet, as mentioned above, the division between external and internal influences of burnout are not as clear-cut as Figure 3 suggests. A blurred or ragged line, as shown in Figure 4, would be more appropriate.

There is little doubt that some organizations – by design or, more usually, by sins of omission, create conditions for burnout. Some jobs by their very nature demand special qualities: dealing with death and dying, for example, or working with sexually abused children. But even here, the organization itself has an important role to play in providing adequate and relevant support services.

Those working in such areas have a right to expect to be provided with:

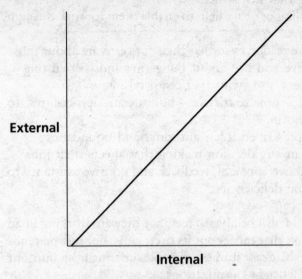

Figure 3: Factors Contributing to Burnout/1

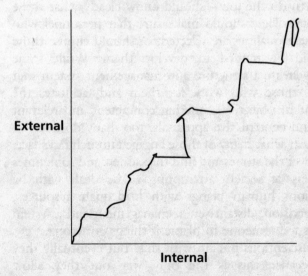

Figure 4: Factors Contributing to Burnout/2

- training that helps them
- counselling or other help to enable them to work through problems
- adequate resources so that their concerns are about those they serve and not about budgeting and cost-cutting
- competent and sympathetic supervision
- efficient – not restrictive – bureaucratic procedures to work within
- clearly prescribed roles, authority and boundaries
- a share in any decision-making that affects their jobs
- constructive appraisal, feedback and positive assistance to overcome deficiencies

They should also be able to feel that they are working in an organization that carries out its overt aims, not just pretends to. Many of the case studies of people suffering from burnout highlight deficient organizations.

Employers – because people of special qualities are necessary to do the job – should know clearly what those qualities are. They should make sure that personnel who possess these qualities are selected, or should choose those who could be trained to develop them. While some employers create a structure and management system that both aids those who work for them and facilitates the attainment of objectives, offering competent and relevant training and constructive appraisals, too many do not.

Remember what many of those engaged in such tasks face. We turn over the stones and find the sadness and sometimes the vileness of society attempting to be dealt with by conscientious human beings with inadequate resources, poor supervision, distant senior management and a system that looks for someone to blame if things go wrong.

The conscientious put up with this. But eventually they break – because this is the only way out they allow themselves. Many enter teaching, social work, nursing and similar occupations with expectations about what could and should be done. These expectations are consolidated during training. They confirm what society expects. But then what they find themselves having to do does not mesh with these ideas. The organization may maintain its public image, but its inner reality is different. So the idealistic become disillusioned.

Then there is the guilt. Many roles are impossible to fulfil. Some aspects have to be sacrificed. The nurse who sees herself as a professional but also as a caring, sensitive person who should have sufficient time and energy to care for all her patients, finds that she has to make choices. The police officer, facing a riot, feels he should be brave but is frightened, and perhaps is even more afraid of admitting he is frightened. The competent teacher feels she should be able to cope with all sorts of difficult children, only to find she cannot. The resourceful social worker who feels that there must be a solution to most problems, when with present resources and economic climate there simply is not. The mother who thinks she should naturally be able to cope with her newborn baby, but whose demands she is unable to meet.

We expect openness but find covert political machinations. We expect our role to be clearly defined but we experience ambiguity. We expect to be developed but find we are manipulated. We expect our organization to be rational, fair and equitable, but too often it is shabby, fumbling and unfair. Our expectations are out of tune with the reality in which we work or live. Although our expectations are a myth, it does not stop us from continuing to try to meet them.

The conscientious attempt the impossible and feel guilty when they fail. If we were our own best friend, we would give ourselves a clear message: 'Get out.' For many the symptoms of burnout are shouting that message. Your body is screaming: '*STOP!* Do *not* continue to live life in this way.'

Individual characteristics that seem to contribute to burnout include:

- tendency to depression
- obsessive-compulsive traits
- over-conscientiousness
- tendency to over-identify with clients/patients
- perfectionism
- low self-esteem
- overdependency
- idealism (which has turned to disillusionment)

Not one of these factors in itself is necessarily the prime cause of burnout. It is more likely that a number of different factors of varying intensities will contribute, as well as certain adverse external conditions.

What do sufferers themselves say about what has caused their problem? Here are some of the reasons they have pin-pointed:

- taking on extra responsibilities
- being depressive by nature
- work overload
- conflict at work
- caring for people who need special attention (e.g. the terminally ill, the elderly, deprived families, etc.)
- inadequate resources
- inadequate training
- responding to crises rather than trying to prevent them before they arise
- feeling isolated and cut off
- lack of competence
- a series of negative events
- becoming disillusioned after going into a profession for idealistic reasons

- lack of peer group support
- poor supervision
- isolated management
- dealing with difficult issues (such as child abuse)

Of course, many of these studies are based on small samples (and they were not randomly selected), so it is not possible to generalize. Nevertheless, case studies do provide an insight into what it feels like to have suffered from burnout.

Here are some case histories, told by burnout sufferers themselves. Take particular notice of the differences as well as the similarities between the stories – they provide a key to some of the symptoms of burnout, but also demonstrate that there is no simple, straightforward pattern that applies to all cases.

NURSES' STORIES

I am 39 years of age. I was a staff nurse for six years before I became a nursing tutor.

I've always enjoyed a busy life. I like things to move fast, and require multiple 'inputs'. I liked working in a practical setting, and was always able to recover from daily stresses once I was away from work. In 1980 I became a tutor to a specialized nursing course. I also started studying part-time and my social activities decreased. Study, taking work home, lectures and note-taking all increased my workload. I shared my job with a workaholic who eventually became ill for a year and then moved abroad. I myself also eventually reached a stage of complete burnout; I was unable to help myself or even see my problem.

I am married with a 16-year-old son. For the past three years I have been suffering from clinical depression, according to my doctor and consultant psychiatrist, but my condition fits the symptoms of burnout exactly. Pressure at work has been the main cause of my breakdown.

I have worked as a nurse for 25 years. For the 11 years prior to my breakdown, I worked three nights a week in a geriatric hospital. The number of staff was gradually reduced and our workload increased dramatically. Staff morale became very low as we had no support at all from management. Looking back to those days, I can see that my breakdown was inevitable – I don't know how I kept going for as long as I did.

I first went to my doctor in October 1988 because I was experiencing chest pains. I suspected that they were stress-related, but I wanted to make sure. I had six months off work and was referred for further treatment, which consisted of antidepressant medication and informal psychotherapy.

I went back to work for 11 months and then had to take further sick leave.

Ten days after returning, I was summoned to see someone from the personnel department and subjected to what I can only call 'harassment'. The story is long and involved, but in July 1990 I resigned from my post and started working three nights per week in a private nursing home for the elderly. I enjoyed the job very much at the start, although I had never worked so hard – an 11-hour shift with barely time for the 45-minute break we were allowed.

However, during the last four months I have found the pressures and stresses are rising again. I have worked for four nights per week since Christmas 1990 in an effort to combat my social and domestic problems, but the plan is backfiring and I am working myself into physical and mental exhaustion.

We have a lot of new patients now who suffer from dementia. The thing that upsets me most is the physical and verbal abuse that we get from well over half our 40 residents. I am totally fed up.

I am stuck between the assistants below me and the head of the nursing home above. I try to keep my staff's morale high, while mine is being pushed below acceptable limits. I am in a 'no-win' situation – how do I tell my boss how I feel without talking myself out of a job?

It seems that no matter how, where or how hard I work, I cannot get much job satisfaction or any support from my superiors. My doctor says I am too much of a perfectionist. I do like to do things properly and I am finding it hard to change my attitude – but I am trying to work on it.

The people who have helped me survive these awful years are the doctors, nurses and fellow patients. My doctor has been wonderful, seeing me for 40 minutes during busy surgery hours and phoning me at home to see that I was OK. My consultant psychiatrist has also given me more time than I could have expected. My informal psychotherapy has also helped, but the doctor who helped me in this way changed her job and the meetings had to end.

After discharge from hospital, I attended a day clinic for four months. At the beginning I went for five days each week, but when I started my new job this was reduced to two days. I still attend a social group one afternoon a week, and I'm getting support from staff and other patients.

My boss is sympathetic, but I am sure that she doesn't realize the pressure I am under, dealing with 30 to 40 confused and often violent patients for 11 hours at a stretch, day after day and week after week – with only two or three assistants to help me.

Working with the elderly is not considered one of the most stressful areas of nursing – maybe it is just me, or my attitude to the job?

This is how Julia Keachie described her own experience of burnout in an article she wrote for the *Nursing Times*:

The unpleasant process of burnout happened to me over a period of two years, despite having a job I loved. I worked as a nurse for nearly 20 years, the last eight as a leg ulcer specialist and research sister in collaboration with the consultant vascular surgeon. I was thrilled to be offered the post and I looked forward to the challenge.

For the first six years I was filled with enthusiasm to help the many patients who had suffered from the misery, pain, smell and social isolation that an ulcerated limb can bring. I had articles published and was invited to speak in Britain and abroad, and organized bus trips for elderly, housebound ulcer patients. I helped to organize a study day and the production of a video, and I also helped to teach district nurses on a nationwide basis, with a patient present. I won a Florence Nightingale award.

I managed a mortgage on my own. I had a good social life and many friends. I helped a friend who raised and trained horses, and however stressed I felt at work, working with the horses always made me feel relaxed.

Disillusion hit me initially in my sixth year. I wanted to set up a training course on the ulcerated limb for nurses, and I approached the school of nursing to ask if this was possible and was prepared to go on a teacher's training course. I was knocked sideways when I was told that I would have to do three or more courses in my own time even to be considered for the necessary training.

Bed closures at my hospital increased. Management became strict about budgets. I had to become downright devious to give patients necessary supplies. There was no point in me assessing patients if I could not give them appropriate supplies.

The final straw was the introduction of a computer to document all my local district house-calls. I did not mind filling out forms but I strongly objected to having to go back to hospital and sit in front of a screen for at least two hours a week.

During this spell, my nursing manager retired and a 'new broom' was soon in the post. She tried to renew my previous enthusiasm and confidence, but it was too late.

Gradually, I found I could not be bothered with anything and every time my bleeper went I hoped it would not be another patient. I found myself using any excuse to go back to the hospital a few times a day and then ended up with a rush of house-calls in the afternoon.

I dreaded the busy out-patients clinic. I felt guilty about my feelings. I had difficulty in sleeping and a tight knot in my chest most of the time.

It came to the crunch when on several occasions I could not make a decision on how best to treat the simplest ulcer.

What changed my life was answering an advertisement for a riding holiday in Arran, Scotland. I fell in love with the island and six months later I answered another advertisement for a job there. I took a part-time position in a nursing home overlooking the sea for a third of the salary I had been used to. I had suffered from burnout and the recovery for me has been slow. In my opinion, for any nurse there are many unnecessary stressful, administrative, non-nursing chores that are time-consuming.

I have suffered from burnout for two years. In retrospect it started in October two years ago, reaching a peak nine months later and then reducing in intensity.

I have my own home, am divorced and have no children. I trained in a large general infirmary, staying there to staff the Renal Unit. I was forced to leave the Unit as a 'solution' to my 'inability to cope'. I transferred to neurology for six months, then left the National Health Service and now work as a night nurse in a hospice.

Many factors led to my burnout. The main problem seemed to be the attitude of the nurse in charge. She was unprofessional, inflexible and unreasonable. She made it clear that she did not care for me personally and regarded me as professionally inferior. The two consultants compounded this; one disliked me because I held an office in the Nurses' Union (he said this made me unreliable); the other refused to speak to me for periods of months and was persistently unpleasant because I voiced my worries concerning a patient to the social worker in charge of the patient's case. This was treated as a breach of confidentiality.

The frustrations of my working life were one of the things which led to the breakdown of my marriage. Then the problems really began!

I sought the help of my manager to deal with the head nurse's behaviour and to help me deal with my work. Initially, I received understanding, but my manager was a personal friend of the head nurse . . .Eventually and inevitably, I made a drug error and despite the fact that I had been seeking help from my manager for three months, she decided to discipline me. She could not accept the fact that I was completely burned out. I was offered no help; no counselling even though the hospital has two counsellors available.

In desperation, I asked to see my Patient Services Manager. I was met with unyielding authority. I had to move voluntarily or be faced with further disciplinary action. There was no acknowledgement of my state, no offer of help.

My only help came from two friends and from my family. One friend realized before I did that I was suicidal and spent a lot of time talking me through it. She and my other friend were simply there: available, understanding, accepting.

My family were unaware of the real depth of the problem – they still are. But they were there when I needed them and would drop everything to travel miles to be with me.

Most of all, time has allowed some of the wounds to heal. There are still occasions when the signs and symptoms return, most notably the paranoia. I have to accept that it is part of me now, that I could not endure the trauma without some lasting change. I am certain that counselling would have helped.

It was not until five months after the worst period that I began to realize what had been happening to me. I had no insight at all. I still find it difficult to talk about. I remain wracked with guilt about having considered suicide, and am in perpetual fear that if it gets that bad again there will be no one there to help me. Later this month I start my BA in Health Care Management. I hope to obtain a management post. None of my staff under my care will be subjected to the uncaring, inhuman approach that I was given.

I have suffered from burnout. It began five years ago, and now the symptoms have begun to improve. I am male, single (living with someone at present whom I have known for 12 years), 33 years of age and have worked in nursing since I was 18. Most of my career has been in community psychiatric nursing. Now I work in post-education and training. I have had my present post for about four years.

What caused it all? Working alone. Absence of clinical supervision. Taking work home – linked strongly with the invasion of my personal time with work-related projects and tasks. Poor understanding on the part of my supervisors. Lack of support, guidance and feedback from supervisors about my performance and general work.

Other factors which contributed included: low level of job-satisfaction at times; poor communication within the system – simple procedures such as ordering goods or stationery were immensely complicated; having had in the whole of my career poor training (really the absence of training) to take on new responsibilities and duties; being left to get on with it in unfamiliar circumstances; and others having very high and unrealistic expectations of me. In addition there were unrealistic deadlines, personal and family problems as well as those related to work, and nowhere to go for personal help within the organization. I turned to alcohol as a way to cope.

How did I manage to get out of it? I took time out. I went for private counselling. I got professional help about my alcohol problem – I now don't drink at all. I admitted that I was burned out, first to a friend and then to a colleague. They were genuine, non-judgemental and accepting. My parents gave me support and understanding. I also found that praise, when I made some improvements, was very helpful.

I became more self-disciplined, and then more assertive. I set time aside for leisure activities. I admitted that some of my and others' expectations were impossible. I began to look after myself more. I planned rewards for myself: meals out, holidays.

I gradually began to improve as I took more control over my life.

SOCIAL WORKERS

It was not until I read the description of burnout that I realized that this is exactly what I am suffering from. I am currently under medical treatment for anxiety attacks, depression and an irritable gastric problem. Stupidly, I pride myself on only having taken one day off sick over the last two months, when this burnout has been building up.

What has contributed to this condition? I qualified last June as a professional social worker. This was a complete change of career for me, with no clearly defined area of social work which I wanted to get into. As my two-year course progressed, I became deeply suspicious of being a local government worker – my four months of practical placement were in a specialist area, not generic, but I was picking up on the particular stresses involved as a generic worker. Because of this, I avoided what most of my colleagues did, that is, sign up for general work within my region, in order to gain the 'magical' two years post-qualifying experience. Instead, I wrote to various drug/alcohol agencies, and as it happened, the agency that offered me a temporary post was with a drug project run by the local government authority.

I spent eight months there, and again, observed through much liaising with general social workers the pressures they were under and the amount of their work that was reactive/crisis intervention rather than proactive and preventive work with clients. A vacancy arose in a health centre, and since I was already experienced in working with multi-disciplines, I thought this would be a side-entrance into the 'dreaded' generic social work which I had at some point to face. There was always a general feeling coming from colleagues that I should be getting general experience, and senior management also advised it.

I got the job and I have been working with one other social

worker, one home-worker, one occupational therapist and one senior social worker for nearly five months now. After two months' 'honeymoon' period, I began to carry a case-load of 30 (this is the average). I am now physically exhausted, I lack confidence, I feel de-skilled, isolated and very frustrated.

The frustration is directed completely at the local authority which employs me. The tension is about what the college said social work was about and the expectations of the local authority and its failure to effect the promises made to newly-qualified social workers. In their adverts they promise regular supervision, support, and opportunities for self-development. In this district this is a pipe-dream.

As time goes on, I am made to feel that I am the problem, that I am not coping, and I can see my supervisor withdrawing from my querying and raising of issues that I feel are neglected. I feel so isolated and misunderstood. I do not have sufficient time to have in-depth counselling with clients, and even I am beginning to adopt the attitude of just dealing with the presenting problem and hoping that the client does not raise other issues. The matter of child abuse is another area that angers me intensely. I am being granted a four-day course – and we are expected to be experts on abuse thereafter!

So all this makes me feel very insecure, inadequate and incompetent. When I ask for extra time to complete reports and case records, I am refused on the grounds that I should be able to do this within working hours.

So how have I been coping? I am taking various pills to keep me sane. The doctor has advised me to find alternative, non-local authority social work if I am not to slip into permanent depression. I have a good support system with my two colleagues. They are equally frustrated. Both are afraid of expressing their difficulties as it is seen as a sign of weakness.

I try to keep a balanced life outside. I exercise two or three times a week, but this fitness is knocked out by my compulsion to eat, which the doctor describes as 'comfort eating'. I don't drink to compensate, and I know my faith in God has helped me through some really dark times. However, body and mind can only withstand so much; I guess I haven't found my niche yet in social work.

I am 36 years old, and made this move to have a more satisfying job. I feel that basic-grade social workers, especially the newly qualified, get a raw deal from my particular local government authority, and I don't accept that this is the way it should be. From my previous experience in commerce, I feel it is not lack of personal resources that is the real problem but serious management incompetence, which leads to their unrealistic expectations.

I am now applying for other jobs.

Over the years I have developed professionally. I have social work qualifications, a degree and a further education teacher's certificate. The local authority I worked for had a progressive reputation. Their policy was brilliant but was in no way implemented in practice. At first I felt that I was effective in my job, but that changed. Things became difficult when a ceiling was put on our budget. We were given additional work. I could hardly cope with 1.5 jobs.

It seemed to start because of a clash with my immediate supervisor. It was exacerbated by lack of support and understanding. It was fuelled by the fact that I had changed offices 18 months previously – the move had been a bad one for me. I had financial problems at home. My parents had recently retired and were at a loose end. Thus my experience of burnout came rather suddenly.

My supervisor and I had a confrontation when I wrote a reference for a team member and he disagreed with the contents; he had pigeon-holed her as being 'no good'. She did have negative aspects professionally but she also had some very positive ways of thinking and working. The anger came from him to me. But I accept that. I knew he would not have written a positive reference. I did not consciously know that I would annoy the man, but I could have predicted his response if I had thought long enough about it.

From that moment my supervisor was unnecessarily critical of everything and looked for ways in which others would agree with his criticisms. As often happens in such cases, there was a conspiracy amongst managers to ignore what was happening. What tipped the balance was a deliberate and calculated programme of professional opposition by my supervisor and collusion with this by colleagues; not because of loyalty to my supervisor but because they felt it was better to be on his side than become his victims.

How did I try to tackle things? I helped myself the best I could. I avoided meetings at which my supervisor was present. I attempted to instigate grievance procedures through my union representative, but because of her fear of the supervisor, she delayed and delayed until it became no longer viable.

There was a time when I was waking up every morning with a headache. I went to my doctor and was put on tranquillizers for the first time in my life. I didn't complete this course of treatment because the tranquillizers made me dozy.

The very worst aspect was that my supervisor (a very intelligent and academically able person) found my Achilles heel. It was a very effective ploy. I value my professional status and reputation, and he found multiple ways of destroying my confidence.

At the time confrontation came to an end (my supervisor left for another job) the only tactic I had left to defend myself was to continue the non-cooperation in the hope that disciplinary proceedings would ensue and I would be able to express my feelings and observations that way.

How did I react to all this? I failed to cope effectively with daily work. As I've said, I had headaches each morning. I coped as well as could be expected. I managed to reach a 'draw' situation with my supervisor, no one winning or losing. At least two others among my colleagues have suffered long-term illnesses after confrontations with that man.

My only real support came from a very brief interaction on the phone with a colleague from my previous job. We had worked so well together and knew each other's strengths and weaknesses in an open and honest way. It was, I suppose, a reassurance that I could work effectively. I had begun to doubt my own skills.

I qualified as a social worker in April 1980 and worked in the same office for just over a year. Initially I worked across the board, then I specialized in working with disturbed adolescents and then spent six years with abused children and their families. For three years I was employed as a specialist, working only with sexually abused youngsters. I did extra training and was used in a consultative and training role, but with no reduction in my case-load. I decided to become self-employed. I then had to accept my own physical and sexual abuse as a child. I realized this had to be dealt with. I found I was paralysed, unable to speak. I was admitted to hospital. The tests showed that my heart was OK. I was told I was suffering from acute stress. I booked myself into a private clinic for two weeks' rest. I seemed calm and sane. Without warning I was confronted with my own feelings (which had been suppressed) in relation to my own abuse.

  I did eventually win through. I am now working in a private residential home using my social work skills in a more caring and protected setting. I will not go back to the mainstream for at least another year.

The main thing that contributed to my burnout was that I was the only worker dealing with survivors of ritualistic abuse. I experienced a sense of isolation. My supervisor kept telling me that survivors of occult abuse were no different from other clients. I knew this was not so. I knew other workers in the same field who felt the same way. My supervisor could not address my feelings because he felt that they were unwarranted. I knew that he could not have coped with some of the horrific incidents I was trying to convey to him. He failed to respond to my distress. Our organization had inadequate guidelines – in administration and case-work practice. So stress just built up. There were few checks. Supervision was inadequate.

I have been in social work for 22 years. I learned to contain my real feelings. I learned to hide my personal stress. My family and Catholic boarding school experiences did not allow me to express a variety of feelings. I had to be 'good and just cope'. This was built into my personality.

For six years I suffered stress. I endured considerable stress due to trauma within my current family. My wife was ill and my parents had to go into residential care. We could not cope with them.

The supervisors I worked with were so damaged and needy that the thought of suicide was ever-present and intense. The horror and menace of what they were sharing created more stress for us all. Society does not want to know. Sometimes prominent people were involved and it was not safe to trust anyone. There were personal threats made against me (including a death threat). I don't know whether it is worse for male workers. I do know that as a man I had to offer some protection to women. But I could not. I felt a failure. I was frustrated. It was difficult to do anything for the abused survivors. They were so terrified during disclosure that at times I had to use physical restraint, as their acting-out behaviour might have led them to harm themselves.

How did I feel? I knew I was overloaded but I constantly denied it to myself. I took on more and more work. The pressure increased. I felt like a train that was out of control. I became blinkered. I could not see the wood for the trees. I could not deal with my stress. Accidents were becoming a major part of my life. I felt so fatigued. Once one of my supervisors had an epileptic fit and fell into a canal 15 foot deep when I was out walking with her. I risked my life trying to save her. She was unconscious. Once down in the canal with her I could not get her out as the wall was too high. Fortunately, we were both rescued by a passer-by. Around the same time I fell through a ceiling at a neighbours' house and damaged my hand by seriously cutting it on a glass coffee table – all due to stress and fatigue.

At a superficial level, I gave the impression that I was coping. This was just a defence mechanism. I was good at pretending. I could not cut off from work. I was on a constant state of alert because of the needs of my clients. The boundaries between work and home became obscure. To hide my anxiety, I took on more commitments. To avoid feeling helpless, I worked most evenings. I cut myself off from the rest of the agency and from my family. I didn't take any time off. I worked weekends.

A disciplinary hearing I had to face stopped me in my tracks. I knew I had been negligent with some of my mileage claims, as well as with some of my administrative tasks (case records). Case records were difficult to maintain because of the sensitive nature of their contents and the fact that members of the occult had broken into our office to try to steal them. The agency was at fault for having inadequate guidelines and procedures.

What helped me? Learning relaxation techniques; sharing my stress in a group with others who faced similar problems; getting feedback from the group; using a competent counsellor; finding someone to understand and believe that I was suffering from stress; getting a good supervisor and finding procedures that assisted and not restricted me.

TEACHERS

I came to this town in 1965 at the age of 28 to teach crafts in two primary schools. For the first time in my career, I loved the work. The schools and town were new and exciting, and the population was a social mix from all areas throughout the UK. My family thought I was in the wrong place, but I was content as I was working with good people. My headmaster went on to become the Head of one of the largest schools in the area, and my boyfriend made a fortune in the oil industry. My work was a rock against considerable family stress and problems.

Fifteen years later I hit burnout.

What contributed to my stress included family illness; uncertain personal relations; a viral infection and the treatment I needed for it; and the fact that without warning I became peripatetic to seven schools – just a letter in the post.

I cracked.

I tried to go back to college to sort myself out. No grant allowed. No security at the end of it. I felt there was no solution.

Finally I insisted on a risky ear operation to overcome the viral infection problems. It worked.

In the meantime my personal relations went down the pan.

Two years later I am on my own. Healthier and coping. I am hanging on for early retirement and thinking of going on to a four-day week next year.

I treat my teaching as a joke. I see too many children – *900* – it is not a satisfying experience – just a rat race. And that's a pity.

I am 44 years old. After getting my degree, I spent ten years in a large London school. It was an all-girls comprehensive (2,000 pupils). I ended up as head of English; then I took an MA; then four years as a senior teacher in a smaller girls' school. I am now the head of a large, expanding, mixed school in another area.

When I had a year's secondment (working 'on loan' to another regional teaching authority) things began to go wrong. It took several years to recover. I found it difficult to cope. I couldn't think straight. I found myself cutting off from others. I was tired.

I work in a hospital tutoring sick children. I've always been a perfectionist. I enjoy being very busy, yet I began to realize that I was a workaholic. My life was eat/sleep/work for 24 hours a day. I was unable to help myself and 'see' the problem. Most of my colleagues were in the same state and adding to each other's burnout. I personally found work colleagues of little help – as I said they were either burned out themselves or unsympathetic and constantly demanding more. I was known as the person who always coped with whatever situation I encountered – others could not cope with me not coping. I felt I just had to suffer the consequences.

How have I managed to improve things? I had a year out to study but still strived for perfection. I am now in a state of 'chronic burnout' – that is, a sort of homoeostatic balance. I struggle in my job to cope with perpetual stress and the need to be innovative and dynamic, generating ideas and absorbing the problems of others but not taking them 'on board'. I have periods when I am on automatic pilot and am able to function at sufficiently high levels to be effective, but I know that I am just riding the storm until I have the energy and drive to be back on top form. I find it easier to work through a situation and regenerate rather than to have time out. I have had this job for five years and I can't remember when I was last off sick. This now is my normal life and part of my make-up, which I have to recognize for what it is and live through; with it; in spite of it. To do a less demanding job would be incompatible with my personal lifestyle and cause even greater stress.

References

S. Capel, 'The incidence of and influences on stress and burnout in secondary school teachers', *British Journal of Educational Psychology*, 57, 1987.

C. Cherniss, 'Observed supervisory behaviour and teacher burnout in special education', *Exceptional Children*, 5.54, 1988.

H. Firth and P. Britton, 'Burnout, absence and turnover amongst British nursing staff', *Journal of Occupational Psychology*, 62, 1989.

B. C. Galser, 'The constant comparative method of qualitative analysis', in G. J. McCall and J. L. Simmons (eds.), *Issues in Participant Observation* (Addison-Wesley, 1969.)

J. Gilmartin, 'Stress in relation to the nurse teacher', unpublished dissertation, 1990.

J. Hare et al., 'Predictors of burnout in professional and paraprofessional nurses working in hospitals and nursing homes', *International Journal of Nursing Studies*, 25.2, 1988.

R. Hughes, 'The emotional cost of nursing', unpublished assignment, 1990.

J. P. Lemkau et al., 'Correlates of burnout among family practice residents', *Journal of Medical Education*, 63, 1988.

C. L. Thompson, 'Stress related to nursing', unpublished assignment, 1991.

3

CUTTING DOWN THE HEAT

MOVING OUT OF BURNOUT

The stories you've read in Chapter 2 are not happy ones. At times, many of those who related them felt without hope. But the important point is that most of them *did* find a way out. This chapter is about how you might do so and begin to take control of your life once again.

There are no panaceas or simple techniques. But there are ways out. Providing you are willing to make decisions and try things out, you can recapture a life worth living and feel again the flow of positive energy as you live and not just drag yourself through each day.

You must accept that you have to take action to improve things. This doesn't mean that burnout is your fault and that you are to blame for your condition. What it does mean is that you cannot rely on anyone else to help – only yourself.

There is a four-point plan of action: stopping the burning, reducing the heat, getting out of the fire and making the heat bearable.

STOP THE BURNING

Your first aim should be to cut yourself off from the pressure – at least for a short while. 'Impossible! Can't be done!', I can hear you shout. But, however difficult your circumstances are, you should be able to get away for at least a weekend. A week is preferable. During this break, do *not* concentrate on your difficulties. Just experience what it is to have a respite. With the break must come a decision to take some action to improve things when you return.

These two actions (your break and the decision to improve things in a limited way) are palliative. That is, they will only relieve symptoms, not deal with deeper issues. But relieving the symptoms is just what you need at this stage.

REDUCE THE HEAT

Find two or three things which would improve your work life. They can be quite small. They might include such things as:

- not working so late every night
- not taking work home
- saying 'No' to others' requests that you do extra work
- having a real break at lunchtime
- cutting out some less essential meetings
- avoiding some of the people who cause you problems
- trying not to be so perfect about everything you have to do
- giving yourself a treat (a music evening, seeing a play, visiting places that interest you, a good meal, a walk in the hills, etc.) once a week

With some of the pressure a bit more under control, it is important that you now spend some time looking more deeply at what you need to do. If you don't, you're likely to slip back into more severe burnout again.

GET OUT OF THE FIRE

Now on to these wider issues. Your problems are likely to have been generated from:

1. within the organization in which you work
2. the nature of the work you do
3. a series of negative events in your life
4. your own personality

These are not necessarily or usually discrete items. They are presented this way for convenience and so you can examine them separately to start with. Later you can look at how they interact.

Before you start, ask yourself where you feel most of the problems lie. Imagine that you have ten points to allocate between the different categories. You could allocate all of them equally (that is, 2.5 points to each) or in any combination you like.

For example, you might have an allocation as follows:

1. within the organization in which you work – 5 points
2. the nature of the work you do – 2 points
3. a series of negative events in your life – 1 point
4. your own personality – 2 points

Later you may want to change your allocation as you read more fully about the implications of each category.

The Organization

Table 1 is a flow chart outlining the decisions you need to make. You may want to return to it as an agenda for your actions.

If you answer 'No' to most of the questions in Table 1,

Table 1

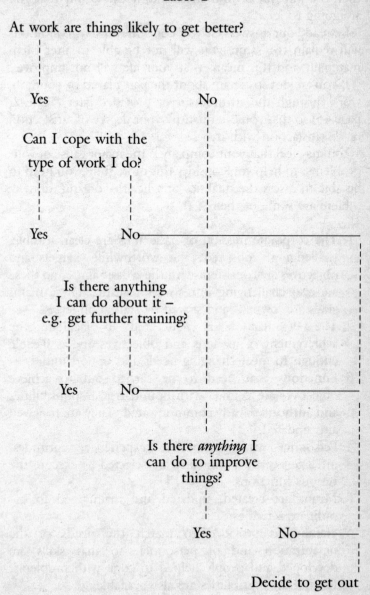

At work are things likely to get better?

Yes   No

Can I cope with the
type of work I do?

Yes   No

Is there anything
I can do about it –
e.g. get further training?

Yes   No

Is there *anything* I
can do to improve
things?

Yes   No

Decide to get out

then the way out of your stress is to decide firmly that you are going to leave.

Re-read your answers. If you continue to stay, conditions will remain the same, you will not be able to alter them materially and this means that your life will not improve.

If you are not so certain about the part played by your job, work through the attitude survey provided later (Table 2, page 46) so that you can quantify your degree of satisfaction or dissatisfaction with it.

You may feel that your company is the major cause of your problems; to help you consider this more fully, you need to be able to assess the qualities of a healthy organization.

Here are some of them:

1. The corporate mission or basic aims are clear, feasible, challenging, consistent and worthwhile. Targets and objectives are consistent with these basic aims, and these are also challenging but always realistic. These major goals are 'owned' and shared by staff at all levels.
2. The organization is structured to facilitate the achievement of its aims and objectives and is flexible enough to meet changing needs and opportunities.
3. Functions that need to be carried out to achieve objectives are defined with boundaries, responsibilities and authority clearly communicated. They are reviewed and updated.
4. Personnel with appropriate experience, aptitudes, intelligence and personality are selected to execute the various functions.
5. Means are created, updated and maintained to co-ordinate activities.
6. Training is provided to match the needs of the organization and of personnel, so that skills are developed and people helped to cope with problems. Promotion possibilities are also available.

7. Managers and supervisors provide leadership, guidance and support: they know when to leave things alone and let subordinates get on with the job and when to intervene. They know when to challenge and when to consolidate.
8. Controls and monitoring are consistent, effective but not restrictive. Feedback is constructive. Individuals are helped to overcome deficiencies. Recognition and rewards feature strongly.
9. Communication is open – downwards, upwards and between peers – and is co-operative, not competitive, between departments and persons.
10. Decision-making is rational and includes appreciation of human factors. Participation and consultation play key parts.
11. Senior management are aware of the problems faced by subordinates and provide support and help.
12. People are provided with adequate resources to do what they are expected to do.

The sick organization or business fails in many of these areas. Policies are unclear and inconsistent: 'We aim to provide the best service available and we aim to maximize our profits.' People are asked to do things which are unlikely to succeed. As results move further from targets, pressure is increased for greater effort. As this fails to work, scapegoats are sought. Insecurity deepens. In some organizations there are rules, which if followed, would mean that little would be done. So they are by-passed. But when things go wrong these rules are used to blame people.

Even when basic policies are reasonable, some companies or organizations are so structured that they are inefficient. Lines of command are too long. Senior management are out of contact with staff. Administrative procedures are restrictive, time-consuming and frustrating. Staff are not selected with sufficient care, and unsuitable staff members are promoted. One inadequate senior manager can create havoc in an otherwise sound organization. Jobs are advertised as 'challenging' where there is little challenge. Highly skilled persons are appointed for posts demanding only limited skills. Consultation is minimal. Senior managers are unaware or unconcerned about the realities faced by subordinates. Help is not provided when it is needed: there are no stress-reduction courses and no counselling arrangements. Few managers go out of their way to thank subordinates for doing a good job. Feedback is non-existent.

An attitude survey (Table 2) is a way of assessing the health of a business or organization. Remember, it only reflects your views. To assess the organization fully, it should be sent to all employees, or at least to a random sample of them at all levels. By completing it you will assess your feelings about where you work.

Attitude Survey

For each question, rate your answers on the following scale:

Table 2

5 – fully agree
4 – partly agree
3 – slightly agree
2 – partly disagree
1 – fully disagree

Score

1. The aims of my organization are clear and consistent.
2. All departments work co-operatively to achieve those aims.
3. Generally, we are provided with adequate resources to achieve our objectives.

4. Our organization is well structured to facilitate *Score* the achievement of objectives.
5. Our organization is flexible to meet change and changing needs.
6. My job function, responsibilities and authority have been clearly communicated to me.
7. The training I receive helps me update my skills and do my job more effectively.
8. Senior managers understand my needs.
9. I am adequately informed about the organization generally and about matters which affect my job specifically.
10. I feel I participate in decisions connected with my job.
11. I feel I am consulted sufficiently about changes in organization policies.
12. I receive adequate recognition for work well done.
13. I receive constructive feedback about my performance.
14. Generally, I enjoy the work I do.
15. I feel that I have adequate skills for the work I have to do.
16. I feel I have reasonable control over how I work.
17. Most people in my organization work co-operatively, not competitively.
18. I feel that I work for competent senior managers.
19. My work provides me with adequate challenge.
20. I feel basically secure in my job.

The maximum score is 100. Very few, if any of us, reach this score. A reasonably healthy score is 50. Below 35 shows deficiencies. 25 and below indicates severe problems.

Take a look at the questions you have graded '1' or '2'.

They show where the main problems lie. Is there a pattern to them? Are most of the lower scores connected with senior management, for instance, or with job security? This will help you assess where action is necessary, and help you decide what might be possible.

Analysing your answers gives you an idea of where you perceive your corporation to be. What it does not do is indicate the importance of certain items to you. A more sophisticated way of assessing these is to allocate an 'importance score' to each item: from 1 – not very important – to 10 – very important, and multiply each answer by this score.

The total score is now best out of 1000. Again, 1000 would be rare and virtually impossible. Over 500 is healthy, below 250 indicates problems.

Negative factors may not be the immediate cause of stress, but as things get worse those of us who are more vulnerable are threatened. As matters further deteriorate, other, more hardy personalities find themselves becoming stressed.

Organizations cannot always be friendly, pleasant places in which to work. Tough decisions may have to be made. Not closing a factory may cause the whole company to go into liquidation. Living in the expectation of redundancy is threatening. It may not be possible to remove this threat, but people can be helped to cope.

Where it is clear that your organization is a prime contributor to what has happened to you, then survival may mean taking a key decision: *to leave*. Remove yourself from its contamination. It has failed you – the employee. It has not made it possible for you to function efficiently to its benefit, yours, or your clients', patients', students' or customers'.

Your decision is the first step. At present you may be uncertain about what you are going to do. But at this stage, the decision itself is important. By taking this decision, you provide yourself with hope. You relieve some immediate tension by placing an end (albeit yet unclear) to your present problems. You may sense the possibility of some movement in your life.

Later, you can look at some of the factors that have brought you to where you are, and perhaps get some value out of your pain.

Chapter 6 helps you look at yourself so that you can consider other possible career paths and how to implement them.

It is worth looking at some of the reasons why you have remained where you are for so long. These may include such things as:

- I'm frightened to move
- I feel I won't get another job
- I feel a duty to stay (to clients, patients, customers, colleagues – or even your boss)
- I feel I can't face the hassle of an upheaval
- I really don't know what to do
- I feel I haven't the energy to cope with change
- I feel that I have commitments to others and must not let them down

Your answers may be different. But the key factor remains: you know things will not improve and your doubts freeze you into inaction.

Lack of energy and being frightened of taking steps to free yourself is understandable. The whole activity is formidable – but it can be broken down into smaller tasks which you should be able to handle. You need to pace yourself. Usually the start is slow, but there comes a time when you begin to feel that you are getting some control over what's happening, that where you want to go is clearer and you begin to feel yourself motivated once again. But this won't happen straight away. You have to start, still feeling unmotivated, and put effort in even when you don't feel like it. It is a great help to find someone who is sympathetic, with whom you can explore your doubts and ideas.

If you like your career but not the specific corporation or organization you are in, your task is to look for similar work elsewhere. You will need to list the things in your present organization that have caused your problems and, as far as you can, check that similar conditions will not repeat themselves. At interviews, ask questions – general and open ones at first and then more specific ones about what you want to know. However skilled you are at interviewing techniques, you can never be certain that your interviewer is telling the whole story or even knows what conditions are like, but by careful interviewing, you can reduce the risk.

If you feel you have to stay despite the problems which you know won't improve, have a look at the pressures that keep you from taking action.

List these and their relative strengths, then place them in a diagram similar to that shown in Figure 5.

The thickness of the arrows suggests their respective strengths. Your next step is to strengthen the positive points for change and weaken the negative ones. If you're uncertain what to do, for the present just play around with the diagram. Leave it and then return to it and see how you would like to alter it. Be honest with yourself.

An important point to remember is that there are always advantages to the disadvantages! Look also at the disadvantages of the positive reasons for change. For example, a desire to live your life constructively may mean shouldering heavy responsibilities. Explore what you mean by 'constructively'. You may find it leads you into the trap of self-sacrifice. Being uncertain of what to do has the advantage of putting off taking many decisions.

The essential message remains: review your work, and if

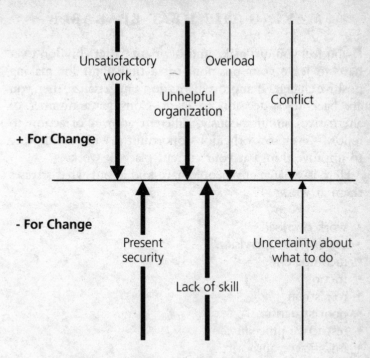

Figure 5: Balancing the Forces For and Against Change

you feel it is unlikely that things will change or that you can change them, you need to decide to get out. There will be regrets, a bereavement for past dreams and hopes, but the decision itself should bring some relief as it opens up a new future. At this stage, the decision is the important point. Life is short. You are wasting your time, your energies and yourself in something that is destroying you. You owe yourself a commitment to provide a satisfying and rewarding life. If your present job fails to deliver this – get out.

What you will have done is to provide some light – just a small one at present – at the end of the tunnel. You will have made your present condition not endless.

MAKING THE HEAT BEARABLE

If you feel you can make improvements, that you don't yet have to leave your position, set a time limit for making positive change. If improvements don't materialize, then you are back to a decision to leave. Consider a number of alternatives simultaneously, different courses of action to follow – even seek other job opportunities while attempting to improve things at your current place of work.

Here is what many people have said about what stresses them at work:

- work overload
- ineffective supervision
- incompetence
- friction
- role strain
- poor structure
- restrictive procedures
- insufficient authority
- inappropriate work
- lack of support

List your main problem areas and what you feel could be done about them. Place a time limit on when you expect results. If things fail to improve, you can first ask what else you could have done, try it and, if you still get nowhere, you return to the option of getting out.

Here are some possible avenues to explore to improve things:

Work Overload

This consists of three types:

1. just too much work
2. work too complex
3. too much variety

These are, of course, made worse by too many interruptions.

Too much work may be a short-term problem, a recurring short-term problem, or a chronic one.

Some of the things you might try include:

- better time management
- better planning
- reorganizing your work
- a fairer allocation of tasks
- delegation (where you are able)
- improving your competencies
- learning to become more assertive and to say 'No'

If, after considering each of these items, you feel that very little could be improved from your end and that things are not just temporary, you need to establish limits and negotiate these with your immediate boss. Make clear what is realistic for him or her to expect from you, what will only partly be done and what it will not be possible to achieve. Explain the reasons for your priorities.

Ineffective Supervision

Supervisors and managers are often judged by three qualities:

1. Competence
   Is this person competent? Does he or she know the job? Understand my problems? Communicate clearly? Plan effectively and allocate work fairly?
2. Trust
   Can I really trust this person? Does he or she carry out

promises? Can I be open with him or her?

3. Compatibility

Do I like this person? Is he or she pleasant to work with?

A competent but untrustworthy boss is unsatisfactory. So is one that you really like and trust but who is not particularly competent.

If you work for one you cannot trust, then all you can really do is to realize this and be careful about what you say and do in case it is misused. In some cases, you can confront your boss about what worries you. But if you work for someone who is very authoritarian, this will not work.

Even if you don't like the person, you may be able to put up with him or her if there is a fair degree of competence and trustworthiness. You might explore what it is you dislike about him or her. People do differ, and such differences can be constructive. A group of enthusiastic extraverts needs the balance of an introvert to get them to think things through. Daring, bold, expedient people need the cautious to keep them in check. Dull, unexciting, conscientious people are useful for completing things. Idealists need the balance of realists; creative people need practical and down-to-earth persons. If you are a good manager, you look for opposing qualities in a team. Perhaps by appreciating the value of your boss' qualities, you might begin to dislike your boss less.

If you work with a boss who is not so competent, you may think through what is not being done so well and encourage more effective behaviour. In this way, you reinforce the positive kinds of action you would prefer. Depending on what sort of person you work for, you might be able to bring these problems into the open.

Incompetence

This is about your own actual or perceived incompetence. Often it is not a general incompetence but is concentrated in one small area. This becomes salient as it stands out from all the other things you do competently.

To help you, you need to list the qualities that would make you better at your job.

You could do it this way:

1. Think of the most competent person you know doing work similar to yours.
2. Now think of yourself.
3. Then think of another competent person.

Take the first and third items: what qualities do these people you perceive as competent share? List these.

Ask yourself how they tackle the problems you find difficult. Is it that you lack training? Practice? Basic aptitudes? First find out how important the tasks are. If they are not so important and only occur occasionally, you may find it OK to lower your standards. If you feel you need training, try to define the essential skills that are necessary, rather than general ones, and specifically those you'd need to combat your problems.

Say your main difficulties are connected with report writing: you spend far too much time battling over what to write and how to express yourself. Take a look at exactly what you do. Do you try to plan, write and edit at the same time? – an almost impossible task. Do you write, edit and then re-edit? Examine what alterations you make. You are likely to find that most of your changes are accounted for by a few categories. Do these changes materially improve your reports or don't they really matter? If they do matter, concentrate on improving your skills only in these areas.

If your problem is connected with planning, isolate what aspects of it cause most problems. Is it decision-making? Not having a realistic timetable? Or not following things through? Do you get in a muddle when priorities change? Concentrate your efforts on improving specific areas.

If you have difficulties dealing with certain types of people, again do an analysis of the kinds of people, in which situations, give you trouble. Is it that you find yourself agreeing to things you'd rather not do, or feel intimidated, or lose your temper? Or can't you express your real feelings? Isolate key features and work on these. Find out what help is available.

Assertiveness training may help. Being assertive is different from being aggressive. It is about letting other people know that you understand their position, and then presenting your own. Assertiveness techniques are explained more fully in Chapter 4.

It is useful to reflect the other person's views. This helps the other person realize that you understand his or her viewpoint:

'I understand that we haven't the resources at present . . .'

'I can quite see that you would rather not discuss this . . .'

Then use the conjunction 'however' and present your views:

'. . . however, there is no way in which I can meet my present goals with present resources, and I want to discuss what I see as my priorities and what will have to be sacrificed.'

Negotiate your priorities if you need to ensure that your overall workload is reduced. Set limits and spell them out. If your boss is unhelpful, spell out what you intend to concentrate on, what will be left partially or completely undone, and put this in writing.

If you have stated your case and your boss does not appear to have got the message, you can use the so-called 'broken-record' technique of repeating your basic statement: 'There is no way in which I can meet my present goals with present resources, and I want to discuss what I see as my priorities and what will have to be sacrificed.' You also need not to take on board the problems of others. This does not mean being unsympathetic. It means letting them know you understand but also being able to say 'No' and not feel guilty. As one social worker said: 'I am fed up with being an "Angel" who takes abuse without complaint.' You also need to become 'fed up' with having to be perfect, with always feeling that you should be there to help others. You, along with the rest, have your rights.

Friction

In many studies, conflict comes out as a major cause of stress. If you find that much of your strain is connected with people (remember some of the case studies in Chapter 2), try to isolate the main elements of the problem. What part did you play? How effective would different behaviour on your part have been? If you know a better way of acting, why is it that you still behave as you do? Trace back through your life to similar situations and see how your behaviour has developed. You are likely to find a pattern. If you want to change, do not meet the problem head on. Take some less threatening situation to try things out on first. Practise mentally before you take the plunge in real life.

There are many courses available in human relations training, including being more assertive, sensitivity training and transactional analysis, which could help.

Sometimes harmony is not so efficient – just more pleasant. As suggested previously, a well-balanced team is made up of people who because of their differing personality characteristics provide constructive conflict.

Meredith Belbin, in a famous study of what makes groups effective, came up with eight necessary group roles. These were:

1. Implementer – someone who turns concepts and ideas into practical plans.
2. Completer – the person who protects the team from making mistakes, looks for aspects of the job that need

more than usual attention, keeps a sense of urgency and makes sure that things are tied up.

3. Co-ordinator – the one who controls the way the team moves towards objectives by using the resources of the team fully.
4. Creative Plant – the person who provides the group with novel ideas and approaches to problems.
5. Resource Investigator – the one who builds links with outside contacts and brings concepts and ideas in so that the team can use them.
6. Team Worker – someone who supports others, listens, underpins weaknesses and works to improve harmony and communications within the group.
7. Shaper – the person who shapes and reshapes the way the group defines objectives and sets priorities; the sort of person who gets the group to change direction.
8. Monitor-evaluator – the one who puts a break on the runaway but exciting group ideas so that decisions are more balanced.

You might guess that some of these roles would need pretty extraverted, confident and independently-minded persons, while other roles require cautious, introverted, somewhat anxious people. The mixture doesn't make a comfortable group but it makes an effective one. Take a look at your conflict. Do you find that people see things differently from you and this annoys you? Maybe their input has value.

Role Strain

Roles are a powerful aspect of your life. They are about power and influence. They are concerned with the way you are expected to behave. Role strain consists of two categories:

1. Role conflict
2. Role ambiguity

Role conflict is about being torn between different demands. You may be working for more than one department with differing needs and priorities. Or for two bosses who expect different things from you. You may see your clients, patients or customers expecting something quite different from what your department expects you to provide. You feel loyalty to your management team but also to your junior staff. As a professional, you feel obliged to act in a certain way, while your organization wants you to cut corners to save costs. You can be pushed in many directions. Doreen is a nurse in a private hospital and has been told that she is responsible for cost-cutting, so that her organization maximizes profits. Doreen feels that she is there to care for patients and not to concern herself with profits.

In some cases, conflict arises from a stereotyped image we have internalized of how we should behave: the nurse – professional and caring, the executive – always able to cope, and so on. We see ourselves acting differently, and feel a failure.

When you are promoted you still feel loyalty to your old colleagues, but now, different priorities are placed before you. You'd like to keep your former colleagues as friends, but you have to implement some unpopular decisions. They don't like it. Neither do you.

Role ambiguity is different. Here you are not certain what you are expected to do. Your job description is vague. It is all-embracing. Ambiguity in a new post is usual. It takes a few weeks to know what's what. When you are promoted you also need time to settle in.

Some of us can tolerate ambiguity and uncertainty. For others it is threatening.

Solutions are not easy. There is no 'objective' way of making decisions. You could bring problems into the open and discuss them with those concerned. You have to 'own' your discomfort.

With ambiguity, you can set boundaries, state how you see things and let others know this is how you are going to operate. Where necessary you can negotiate.

Poor Structure

It is doubtful whether there is ever a perfect structure in any enterprise. Even if there is, it is likely to hinder future development. All you may be able to do is to show where things are not operating effectively, spell out the consequences and what you think could be done.

Restrictive Procedures

Again, little can be done except to spell out the consequences. Make certain that you don't fall into a trap of ignoring rules to get things done (with the tacit agreement of management), only for those rules to be applied to you when you make a mistake. Explain how you intend to operate or what will be lost if you follow rules strictly.

Insufficient Authority

Here you can only present proposals to management. Present them so that the benefits to the organization, and not just to you, are stressed.

Inappropriate Work

Here, you have to weigh up the advantages of what you've got against the disadvantages of feeling underfulfilled. Your best aim is to plan to find more suitable work either within or outside your present organization. Chapter 6 helps you look at your skills, attitudes and abilities and to relate them to possible alternative career paths.

Lack of Support

Present proposals about what you need. Point out what the organization is losing. Stress the consequences. Compare what support you get with what is available in similar organizations. Consider forming a peer support group.

Other techniques that help include:

Using the 'Stopping' technique. If your aim is to stop thinking about work problems when you've left your work place, then every time you start to think of work say to yourself; 'Stop – I refuse to consider work outside the office.' You may need to repeat this 80 times each evening. If you don't do this, however, the first thought about work leads to another and then another and so on, until you're back in your job – at least in your mind. You begin to recapture the stress of your work-related problems and your evening rest fails to refresh you. You don't sleep too well and return to work even more tired. You can use this technique for other aspects of your life, any time that you find yourself having negative thoughts about your family life, lifestyle, or personality traits.

Take care of yourself. Exercise. Eat a healthy diet. Cut out smoking. Reduce your alcohol intake. Take time to do some of things you enjoy doing: walking, woodwork, gardening, going to the theatre, listening to music. Get some more balance in your life.

Learn to relax. See Chapter 4 on how to relax.

Find your stability zones. These are areas, rituals and routines that help you feel secure and safe. It may be listening to music, retreating to a park at lunchtime, working in your garden, walking along a riverside, sitting quietly in a church, walking along the seashore or in open countryside, having a long, leisurely bath, sailing or cruising down a river, watching animals at play, cycling, doing crosswords, polishing silver, being completely alone or being with others you really like, watching comedy programmes on television. You need to seek what suits you and build times into your life when you move into your stability zones. Of course, such activities are palliative only. They won't cure basic problems – but they do help you to cope with the pressure.

Whether you are a health worker, executive, student or politician, the methods for cooling burnout are virtually identical. If things are unlikely to change and you feel that you are unable to influence them in any significant way; then decide to get out. While you are considering where to go and how to manage the process, do what you can to cut excessive work and place boundaries between time for yourself and the other demands on your life. You're a high-powered executive? You may have to sacrifice status but in return you could reward yourself with a life that provides much more of what you want and need.

Most of this applies to small business owners, but additionally, you may need the help of a small business expert to assess the survival potential of your company and how you could improve things. For those with businesses in the UK there are Government-sponsored services that provide helpful business counselling; the first few sessions are free, and more detailed consultancy is subsidized.

One client of mine ran a small business restoring antiques. He borrowed heavily from his bank, which insisted that he pay crippling interest and presented him with impossible deadlines for repayments. He worked from six in the morning until seven at night, six days a week. His marriage was deteriorating rapidly. He was usually exhausted, often ill and each evening drank two bottles of wine in an attempt to blot out his troubles. His drinking didn't help his health or his money problems.

His way out was to renegotiate the repayment period of his bank loan, cut his working hours, get some business advice on how to concentrate on the more profitable aspects of his craft and operate much stricter credit control. When the immediate pressures were off, he was able to work through some the problems connected with his marriage, but as these were deep-rooted and preceded his business problems, it remains doubtful whether the marriage will survive. He has managed to reduce his drinking, however.

If you are a home carer, you need to find some way to get regular breaks, to pace yourself and to have some space for your own life – you need to do this, even if it is to the limited detriment of the person for whom you are caring. Ask relatives, neighbours, social services, voluntary groups, the local church and other organizations for help. There is usually some at hand. It won't remove the main problem but it will make it easier for you to cope. You do not have to carry the whole burden yourself.

If your problems are about your relationship with your partner, the first step is to discuss openly what each of you expects from each other. Just listen – without interruptions. Make sure each of you understands the other's needs and expectations. Don't aim at a compromise which covers over the conflict. See what potential there is in the relationship that is worth investing in for the genuine benefit of both of you. If there isn't anything – then parting is preferable.

COMBATING WORK STRESS

Organizations do not exist to be friendly, kind or nice. They exist to fulfil a mission. Their mission may be clear or vague, obvious or covert; sometimes what is stated is very different in practice.

The nature of some work is not easy for those doing it: hospitals are for the sick, coal mines for extracting coal, hospices deal with the dying. If you work in a hospital emergency casualty unit you have to handle horrific injuries.

Being employed in a business that has to compete in increasingly tough economic conditions means coping with cost-cutting exercises, facing redundancy, and job insecurity.

The intrinsic nature of some tasks is stressful. Personnel need to be carefully selected, trained and given adequate support. An enterprise that needs people who care, are sympathetic and sensitive should provide competent supervision, adequate resources and support. Otherwise idealism and conscientiousness are destroyed.

A very large question you have to face is whether you wish to continue in the same type of work, if it is the work itself that is stressful. Your image of what you personally could do may have been shattered; or you may find the personal price you have to pay is too high. Your life may have been about being a nurse, advertising executive or teacher of mentally handicapped children. But you may have to face up to the fact that you cannot continue to use your energies in this way.

You need to face this quite firmly. It means redefining who you are and what your life is about.

One way of examining this is to look at what 'constructs' you have about a subject. Constructs may be thought of as units of meaning. To handle the physical, social and mental environment, we need to split our world into 'chunks'. Of course, these 'chunks' are not reality itself, only our interpretation of it. We create labels, and although they correspond symbolically with reality, they are artificial. They are our map, not the actual landscape. But it is a map we need to guide us through living. Some maps are somewhat inaccurate, others unclear and still others can become outdated. Some ways of seeing things – some constructs – are more useful than others.

Constructs are also bipolar. Both poles help explain something of the richness of meaning we have for things. Just one pole could not express an idea precisely enough.

Some constructs we share with other people (commonality), some we do not share but can understand in other people (sociality), while others are unique to us (individuality).

Here are some examples in which one part of a construct's pole remains the same while the other changes:

- love<->being alone
- love<->being safe
- love<->indifference
- love<->depression
- love<->freedom

The so-called 'opposite' pole tells us what a person means by the idea of 'love'. Our constructs are not static; they can change with experience.

Now it's your turn to look at some of the constructs you have about your present employment. As in the example above, you will be looking for the opposite poles of the ideas that first emerge.

Note down why you went into your present profession: what did you want to achieve? You may write something like: 'To do something worthwhile.'

Now write its opposite (for you). Possibly it will be: 'Just earning a living'.

Ask yourself again why it is so important for you to do something worthwhile.

You may reply: 'Because that is what my life is about.' This is a core construct, and this is what you will be changing if you give up your profession. This is why it will not be easy for you.

Take a look at the advantages of just earning a living.
You might think:

- more money

- less strain
- time for myself
- time for my family
- time to develop myself in other ways
- less feeling I am bashing my head against a brick wall
- feeling less tired
- being less irritable

Consider also the advantages of doing something somewhat less worthwhile:

- less commitment
- not feeling guilty when I fail
- not feeling I can never do enough
- not being trapped by obligations

Only you can make the choice. If you look at the positive aspects of 'just earning a living', it might be possible for you to reorganize part of your present job so that you gain some of these satisfactions: less strain – pace yourself better; some research suggests that if we have a break before we are too tired, we work more effectively and longer. If we wait until we are really tired, the break has no value. Some of us can last three hours without a break, others only half an hour; find out what your natural work pattern is and work within it.

You could make certain that you have time for yourself and for your family. Of course, there are always pressing reasons why you can't, but in the long run, you are more use to your organization if you are mentally and physically fit. Your family will also appreciate you more. Getting more balance in your life may also be important in restimulating you and providing you with a sense of proportion. Cutting strain and reducing stress can be achieved by looking at what stresses you and by learning how to relax; Chapters 4 and 5 will help you with these points.

If you decide to stay within your profession despite its drawbacks, you will need to take control over some of these adverse factors. You will need to learn to cut yourself off from work when you go home; you'll need to set clear boundaries for what you can and cannot do. It is helpful to form a support network of persons with similar difficulties to yours so that all can share problems and support one another. Why not be the one who takes the initiative for some of these suggestions? Sometimes the cage you feel trapped in can be broken by just believing it is possible.

In the caring professions, the balance between being a detached professional and a sympathetic human being is a difficult one. Many, who have become too involved and empathize by suffering with patients, find the pain and sorrow too much to bear. When a patient dies, the loss is felt as a very personal one. There comes a time for most of us when this becomes too much. This is when so-called 'depersonalization' takes over. We operate without feelings; patients and clients are almost objects to us. We feel dead inside. This is our safety mechanism. We haven't time to listen to a patient who needs to talk, or gently tell someone he or she is dying. We may sense our lack of compassion and feel guilty.

Others are afraid to show their feelings or even admit how they feel to themselves. In one US study, nurses looking after the terminally ill could not cope with the demands of all those who needed help, so they developed a system of priorities based on 'loss differentials' – that is, the value they felt the patient had as a person – and allocated their time accordingly. They didn't work this out consciously, but that's how it turned out they were operating – it was impossible for them to deal with everyone's needs at all times.

What does help is to move from a two-dimensional choice of professional or carer to a three-dimensional one that additionally includes yourself, so that your needs are met and you build in time and activities to recuperate.

Don't deny your feelings. When you feel sorrow, you feel sorrow; denying or repressing it does not take it away. Feel your feelings. Otherwise they fester inside you. Share your feelings with others. Talk over your problems with colleagues. Form a group for this purpose if possible. Also, admit to the so-called negative feelings – such as anger. These are real within you and they powerfully express what you feel.

What helps:

1. Having good supervision
2. Being part of a team that finds time to work through such issues
3. Giving yourself a respite
4. Realizing that you cannot do all you feel you should do
5. Realizing that the system is inadequate for what needs to be done. It shouldn't be – but it is
6. Creating compensatory interests
7. Looking after yourself physically: exercise, eat a healthy diet, moderate drinking and cut out smoking
8. Remembering that making a mistake does not make you a failure; in some cases, only with hindsight could you have acted differently
9. Cutting your work out of your system when you leave for the day
10. Finding out what is reasonable and feasible for you. Know your own limitations. Judge yourself against yourself rather than against what a few 'super-humans' appear to be able to do
11. Pushing to get training to improve competencies that are relevant to your work, asking for what you want out of courses, not accepting clever-sounding techniques that provide perfect answers – there aren't any

12. Learning a form of relaxation or meditation. You might find that you reach a point of stillness within you
13. Believing that you are creative, and looking for innovative ways to deal with problems
14. Listening to yourself, your moods, those fleeting glimpses of something different within you, recurrent dreams, your intuition, those aspects of your personality which surprise you

A brief respite and some immediate reduction in pressure provides a breathing space, but unless you tackle major issues, you are likely to revert to your previous negative lifestyle.

Make an inventory of your positive qualities. What has kept you going? What has enabled you to cope for so long? Your list may include such items as:

- persistence
- loyalty
- sense of duty
- inner toughness
- dependability

As previously suggested, such qualities have a negative aspect. Persistence, loyalty, duty and dependability mean that you hold on to your life only for others. You refuse to give up and move forward, so you remain stuck. This does not mean that if you move on you will have to sacrifice all these qualities. They are important resources of yours. You will need them as you move forward in your life. What it does mean is that you learn to use them somewhat differently. More importantly, you learn when to apply them. There is a time for duty. But there must also be a time for yourself. Persistence is valuable, but so is letting go in certain circumstances to conserve energy and time and reduce hassle.

Our very strengths can be our weaknesses. And the other way round. It can be valuable to express anger, take time off and get out of something too difficult to handle.

If you were your own son or daughter, what advice would you give? Try playing the two roles: you as yourself; you as your (adult) child. Talk things through. You might be surprised about how wise you are.

If you asked the wisest person you can think of (real or fictional) for advice, what would he or she suggest you do? What would you be doing with your life, if you did not have your present problems? What are the things you like doing, that present circumstances keep you from doing? If you had the capacity to manage things better, what would you be doing? What's stopping you doing what you know should be done? What changes would you really like to see? Your answers may reflect immediate needs. You might reply: 'I'd like to get away from it all,' 'Seek rest, have no commitments and never see that place again.' That's fine. And after you've rested – where to then? Ask yourself where you would like to be in five years' time. Doing what? Your answers will help you explore potential futures for yourself.

It is not only those in the caring professions who suffer from burnout. Many mothers bringing up children on a limited income and perhaps without the support of a partner feel the strain; as do those having to put almost every hour of the day into running a small business in times of recession and worrying about the increasing mountain of debt.

Burnout also affects those in larger business organizations. As technology advances, bureaucracy – in theory at least – becomes more efficient. Management information systems operate more sensitively and more quickly. Such systems have their adverse sides. When we are overloaded our initial reaction is to prioritize. We select more urgent and important work and downgrade the rest. Modern information systems pick up the fact that some aspects of our jobs are getting left behind. We are pressed to improve things, so rearrange our priorities, giving in to the greatest pressure. But soon, what we've still left undone gets noticed, and so on until we are forced to attempt everything.

To do this, we trade quality for quantity. We do everything but not to a very high standard. The system soon picks this up and we are informed. Quality control circles are formed and we are made to realize that quality is important in our organization and that we are responsible for the quality of our work. We may even become enthusiastic. We now have to meet both quantity and quality deadlines, and something else has to give. The final way to cope is to reduce the time we spend with people, coaching, training, helping, supervising and motivating. We see our staff less often. We are too pressed to deal with their problems. Of course, motivation falls, labour turnover rises, sickness rates increase along with other problems in our department. In many management systems, employee morale is measured. Senior management is alerted to the fall in human relations concern. Result: a rush of motivation and human relations training. We are reminded that people are the most important asset in any enterprise.

For us, the trap is now complete. We must produce results – quality and quantity – and care for people.

The way out is via stress to burnout to physical illness. When we are ill we play the role of the 'sick person', we are allowed to do many of the things forbidden otherwise; we don't even have to come in to work, we can relax – and we receive sympathy. Eventually we are recycled and the process starts again.

Let's return to an earlier point, and look at it in more detail. How do people react to stress? The usual reaction is fight or flight. But sometimes both seem impossible. If you fight, you know you'll lose. And you feel you cannot flee or retreat. You are left with a third option: to 'freeze' in inaction. Being conscientious, you are likely to try to force yourself onward. But your efforts are now more of a ritual, just an attempt to push yourself through each day. You are working harder with fewer results, feeling exhausted and cut off from others – the classic symptoms of burnout.

This is the price you pay. So it is worth seeing how you can reduce what contributes to your stress. If you cannot, you may have to remove yourself from the environment that is harming you.

Burnout and stress can lead to physical illnesses: headaches, back ache, stomach problems and coronary heart disease.

Many stressed persons still try and push themselves, despite having the additional burden of their physical illness to contend with, as well as the normal pressures. Does the illness have to be so severe that it forces you to do something to reduce or limit what is causing your stress? Your body is definitely trying to tell you something.

What have others said about how they tackle their problems? Here are some of their comments.

A Teacher's Story

I found myself struggling through a particularly difficult phase, when the coping strategies which normally served me well were suddenly ineffective. 'Burnout' was the phrase which came to mind as it described exactly the state I was in.

Several factors contributed to this over a period of time. The principal one being the continuing demands of an excessive workload which moved from positive motivation for three years, through neutrality, to withdrawal of support and direction. I was the school co-ordinator of a five-year project which fought the adding on of more and more elements to an already-overburdened school curriculum. As 'middle-management' I had no authority to influence school policy (as opposed to project policy, where I had generous freedom) and the vision of a changed curriculum was not practically shared.

Naming the feeling and assessing the situation did enable me to reverse the process, but this corresponded with family and financial struggles and out-of-school commitments (I am and was involved in church work along pastoral and adult educational lines). Coming to terms with the 'death and burial' of the project, working through a grieving process, being thankful for the benefits brought to pupils involved in its passing and 'letting go' enabled me to change any remnants of attitudes which would have been destructive.

Resuming work as a full-time English teacher after being a half-time co-ordinator required some active rebuilding of confidence. Since I started teaching only in 1976 and the project began in 1983, I had moved very rapidly in 'personal development and growth' in a short space of time. As frequently occurs: on looking round you find yourself alone!

My age was an advantage; I am now 51 years old, and having weathered many storms, was a able to recognize the experience as yet another that would pass! No doubt, regarding myself (somewhere amidst all the confusion) as a reasonably well-balanced human being with a healthy perspective on life kept me going at times. I am also a Christian and my faith has changed and grown (with its own challenges and difficulties).

Imagination helped me considerably. I felt like an empty shell, but this conflicted with my beliefs. Fighting through activity (painting, guitar playing, swimming – all diversion strategies from past, overloaded crises) was futile, so I gave myself permission to do nothing and be nothing. I did no school preparation, the minimum of any inescapable obligations (shopping, house work etc.) and kept a low profile.

I cannot pretend that the restoration was easy or rapid. It is three years ago now and details become lost in the mists of time. There is nothing like teaching in a difficult school to take your mind off problems, but the personal demands could exacerbate burnout; I think I was rather mechanical in the classroom at first, but I enjoy teaching, entered the profession to teach (having worked in commerce and industry I had no ambition to rise (or fall) to senior management), and believe that this is where my best strength lies. My success in a management role led to encouragement to develop this and apply for senior management posts, but age and gender are still insurmountable obstacles when combined.

Perhaps the turning-point came when I did not get the assistant head teaching post for which I was interviewed. In the debriefing the education officer told me that I was away and above the best candidate, was his and the school governor's first choice, and that he was reluctant and disappointed to tell me I had been unsuccessful. The post went to a younger, male, internal candidate (demanded by the Head of the school). I was probably more relieved than anything – he also told me to continue applying, that I had enough 'time left' and that I would make an excellent head teacher, given time.

Solace – but it made me face the issues – where am I going and why? I had experienced five years of – in my view – unhelpful management from various quarters, political manoeuvrings and what I can only describe as incompetence. I had no desire to spend my remaining ten years at work unprofitably, so re-diverted my focus onto the classroom.

Other warning signals were already on the horizon: I had 'grown into' the first stages of nationwide changes in the teaching curriculum. Having worked intensively through many changes, managed budgets, written exams and taught courses, devised core curriculums, managed and run non-work experiences with unique preparation and follow-up programmes (all gone!), I was well-prepared for the conflicts and crises of impending change.

Already, I am hearing of personal problems from teachers, brought about by the folly of the nationwide curriculum changes – stress, confusion, families suffering and breaking up. The fabric of society is beginning to crack as a consequence of the vain and pompous attempt by the government to regulate what it is impossible to standardize.

So I shall continue to help 11-to-12-year-olds struggle to learn the alphabet (with guitar accompaniment), use my ingenuity to find some piece of literature to captivate video-soaked adolescents and devise strategies to communicate sensitivity to the desensitized, as well as encourage and direct the high-flyers, and control and offer learning to the neglected in the middle.

I have a source of mutual support from other colleagues, particularly my head of department, who has a sound grasp of reality. A developing sense of humour is essential. Burnout? We need to be pruned back to sprout new shoots and grow through the pain.

There are many facets to the way this woman worked through her experience of burnout. She talks of not having to live up to the expectations of others, how she revised her expectations of what her life was about and how she reduced her workload.

A Hospital Social Worker

I am a social worker in a large, postgraduate teaching hospital. I started social work in 1972 with a BA degree in Social Studies but I have no professional qualifications. I was then aged 35, divorced with two young children, middle-class, very naïve and keen, and knew nothing about the vast number of problems I would have to deal with. The abuse within families, the extent of mental ill-health, the continuing poverty level of families – often three generations of the same family were clients and the cycle of deprivation was ever-present. There was gross unemployment. There was little hope for school-leavers. Apathy prevailed and I gradually got stuck into this depression and apathy. I lived in a nice middle-class area.

My burnout was obvious to me – frequent days off work, ill-health (sore throats, colds and feelings of apathy). I felt I was becoming increasingly inefficient. The internal problems at work did not help. One of my supervisors recently retired early, at 50, after he'd gone a bit bizarre – he used to sit under his desk with a woolly hat on his head. The Area Officer dismissed a devoted Team Leader and then went on sick-leave himself for six months. He returned for one week and then walked out, saying 'never again'.

At the age of 49, I seriously considered opting out of social work but then unexpectedly came into some money which gave me choices. I decided to continue my job a little longer, though no longer totally dependent on it for my income. I moved to a new area, and after four years I am reasonably happy. The problems I now deal with professionally concern sudden illness – I deal with sudden loss and not with poverty, unemployment or the cycle of deprivation. This is more satisfying.

I work within a multi-racial community. There are problems of homelessness, new immigrants, language and cultures previously not known to me. I am able to use my first language (an Eastern European one) which is greatly in demand in the hospital. I have my own office. The pay is still rotten and the holidays insufficient.

I have excluded myself from childcare work, which was once a great source of stress to me, and concentrate on the elderly and on mental health work. I am sent on various courses that give me insight and keep me going. I nearly quit social work for good four years ago – which would have been a pity. I often hear of cases of burnout in my old place. They work in a large, impersonal office with a strange bureaucratic atmosphere. I certainly did not fit in there.

Does burnout only affect those in the caring professions? The answer is decidedly no! Competition in a tough market forces businesses to achieve more with less – and not just retain quality but improve it. This reality – logical in theory – can become a nightmare in reality for some employees. Many organizations do not select staff with sufficient care so that the right 'mix' for the job is available. Few provide adequate counselling back-up for staff who cannot cope and are on the verge of burnout.

Employees are left to get on with it the best they can until it becomes too much. The result: stress and burnout. Finally action is taken – usually to get rid of the 'underperforming employee'. Work pressures can add to the demands of home life. The next two case studies concern burnout connected primarily with work, and how work and home interact.

An Electronics Engineer

John was in his late forties. He'd worked for his company for over 20 years. He specialized in computers. Five years ago (because of his success record) he was offered promotion to manager of a department dealing with major clients. He enjoyed what he had been doing, and dreaded the thought of becoming a manager, but felt he had to accept. Anyway, the extra money would be really helpful to family finances. He also liked the idea of the enhanced status.

John wasn't a good engineer – he was brilliant. But as a manager, he lacked about every quality that was necessary, except one: he was conscientious. It was his con-scientiousness that kept him going for five years. Despite loathing almost every day, he stuck at it. He felt he couldn't let the company down. When things went wrong, as they frequently did, John just put in even more effort.

John was slightly introverted, not totally withdrawn but reserved. He appeared rather aloof but in fact he was shy. John had always been shy. As a child an unfortunate accident had left him with a limp. He felt awkward. Not that most people noticed – but John did. He felt ungainly and he dealt with this by becoming something of a loner. John felt it was especially unfair because his disability was not so obvious that others would label him as 'disabled' and treat him as such. No, they expected him to keep up with them when they walked quickly. His physical stamina was less than that of other people but he was expected to put in as much effort as the rest of the staff. This John did. The price he paid was becoming – and remaining – tired.

John was also somewhat submissive. He found it safer to fit in with what others wanted rather than stick up for what he felt was right. The problem was that he could not please everybody; giving in to one meant displeasing another. This didn't matter so much when John was a specialist without managerial responsibilities. He'd put his report in and let others make the decisions. They, then, had the challenge of implementing his proposals.

Now the responsibilities were his. He had to motivate staff. He had to make unpopular decisions – and see that they were carried out. He found that he was getting into more and more difficult situations. John found it difficult to trust people. He became suspicious of their motives and quick to take offence, but he wouldn't confront them openly. His anger remained trapped inside. In this way, he didn't offend and could feel that he was still part of the team. But John almost always felt an outsider.

John felt insecure. He was often depressed. He was sensitive to people's approval or disapproval. He never discussed his problems. Like his anger, they remained locked inside. If his manager asked John how it was going, John inevitably said; 'Oh, fine thanks; no problem.' His manager did not quite believe him but it was easier not to delve too deeply. John felt a strong sense of obligation to others and he was conscientious, persevering and determined. He felt responsible, almost dominated by a sense of duty. This made him carry on despite his pain and his knowledge that the job was not for him.

John's inner tension meant he rarely relaxed. Certainly this gave him an inner drive which made him try to make an uncertain world more certain – but it never really worked. The world, in John's eyes, remained the same uncertain place. He felt something dreadful was going to happen. He was easily perturbed and he would brood, reliving imagined hurts again and again.

John lived alone in a reasonably pleasant flat, but he kept himself to himself. He had been married once but that had not worked out. John felt he would never enter such a relationship again. It was safer to remain alone.

What had John got in his favour? He was qualified, experienced and had a good aptitude for the technical aspects of his work. He was very intelligent. He was imaginative, although he generally tried to stick with tried ideas rather than taking risks with new possibilities. He was reliable and he kept his emotions under control.

What did John's job need? It needed someone who was an extravert, who could mix easily with others, but who was tough enough to push through unpopular decisions without being personally upset each time. It needed someone who was assertive, enthusiastic, bold, open to change and self-assured. These, John was not. Not only did John lack the qualities needed but he had many qualities which were counterproductive.

John wanted to be able to get on with his work without interference and then just pass over his plans for others to carry out without people getting in the way. He wanted clear lines of authority. But these were unclear and he spent hours worrying about whether he should have taken certain action. He wanted to concentrate on the task and not have to manage people. He wanted enough time to do things thoroughly instead of the frequent panics to get things done on time. He didn't want to feel mentally and emotionally drained at the end of each day. He spent most weekends in bed, yet this enforced rest didn't seem to help. He was not getting what he wanted, and getting a lot of what he did not want.

John's case may have been somewhat different from the

more dramatic traumas of the social workers and nurses. But the outcome was the same: becoming even more cut off from people, feeling that he was achieving little despite putting in more and more effort, plus physical and mental exhaustion.

What was John's way out? Of course, you could say that he could modify his personality – and that might have been possible within limits. But the key factor was that John was in the wrong job. He needed to get out. He needed to find employment that suited his personality and his attributes. First, he needed to rest and relax. Later, when he'd re-established himself, he needed to re-examine things more deeply – for example, how he felt about his 'disability'. He needed to learn to value the so-called 'negative' aspects of his character. It's OK to be shy. It's OK to be a loner, if this is what you want. John had important good qualities: conscientiousness, intelligence and imagination. All these, in the right job, would make John a valuable employee and help him realize his basic worth as a person.

Work vs. Home

I am a straightforward person – which is not always an advantage. I expect other people to treat me as I treat them, but this doesn't always happen. People let me down but I still go on trusting.

I am concerned about the role of women in society. I would like things to be more equal. While I was living with Henry, the pressure was on me to get married, have children, become a family and of course give up work. Even then it was not the way I wanted to live. It was constricting and repetitive. I felt that this would be the outcome of all future relationships. Henry could not accept the fact that I still wanted my own life. To his way of thinking I had to be there to cook regular meals, wash his clothes, look after him and carry on working only until I had children. All this at the end of the eighties – has anything really changed? I didn't want to continue looking after him so that he could come home, sit down, have a drink and find the dinner waiting.

When I decided I needed a cleaner, there was strong opposition from Henry. He didn't want somebody coming into *his* house, looking through *his* things. I tried to explain how I felt, how working full-time and looking after the house left no time for my own life. But that was exactly what he wanted.

Work was another area of conflict. I work hard and get paid by results, but the company tends to be anti-women. They employ them but they don't promote them – that's 'jobs for the boys'. Merit doesn't come into it. I found it terribly frustrating and often vented my anger on somebody in the office, although usually in the form of complaining about something else.

I needed to leave the job and Henry. I felt angry and worn out.

Leaving Henry was painful. He shouted, he argued, he pleaded, he threatened and when he realized that nothing would make me change my mind, he virtually threw me out. As we weren't married and I hadn't contributed to the purchase of the flat, I was left with nothing. I stayed with friends and then got a one-room flat of my own. Meanwhile things got worse at work. My boss piled on the work. He didn't make it clear what he wanted, so he was able to catch me out frequently. Deadlines followed deadlines without a break. The company wasn't that well organized. It didn't think out what it wanted. Things were changed again and again. They had no idea what extra work was involved. I tried to talk things over with my boss but he'd trot out the old cliché of 'if you can't stand the heat get out of the kitchen.' By this time my stress level was boiling over. I moved from rage to just feeling frightened. My assessments declined. I got no real help other than to be told to get my act together.

I was then made redundant. It was just an excuse to get rid of me. I was without a real home and without a job. I had few friends (and I'd sponged off them enough anyway). I was frightened, lonely and angry. The anger was the worst. It seemed to burn me up as if there were a fire inside me. I had a succession of part-time jobs – none of them satisfactory. I became more depressed. I would just stay in most of the time. I felt ugly, unwanted and useless. I felt drained of energy. To even post a letter seemed too much. I seemed to achieve nothing. Yet underneath it all I felt I had potential if only I knew in which direction to go. My doctor supplied the usual pills and I admit I tended to drink too much. I felt totally stuck.

This woman's problems were about not being able to be herself and not being treated as a person in her own right – both at work and at home. They also concerned unclear objectives, poor supervision, work overload and difficult personal relations at home and at work – and then the final blow of redundancy. This left her pretty low and suffering the typical symptoms of burnout: feeling cut off from others, lack of achievement and mental and physical fatigue.

She did eventually find a way out. Her way was charting what career she really wanted and realizing that she could get some control over her life by taking things at a pace she felt she could cope with. She became a mature student and began to use her undoubted intellect. It wasn't easy but it worked for her.

Here are some extracts from others who have worked their way out of burnout:

Nursing Tutor

Being aware of situations that stress me; recognition of burnout, acceptance of 'perfectionism' and learning to live with it; living on my own with space to move, be myself and not have to live up to others' expectations; having personal friends away from the job; outside activities, personal faith; not taking work home; realistic goal-setting; looking at what I have achieved rather than what I have failed in.

Geriatric Nurse

Taking six months off work; getting professional help (long-term psychotherapy); working part-time.

Social Worker

Realizing that I am the problem and I need to get to grips with things; getting medical help; setting up a support network of colleagues within the organization; exercising two or three times a week; having faith in God; making a decision to find alternative work.

Teacher

Getting medical treatment for a long-standing complaint; treating my job as something of a joke; taking a leave of absence.

Hospital Social Worker

Changing my job; excluding myself from work which has caused me stress in the past; updating my skills through training.

Senior Education Welfare Officer

Developing myself professionally; moving to a different post.

Deputy School Headmistress

Moving jobs to a new and thriving school, and having learned from living through experiences of burnout.

Social Worker (working with adolescents)

Leaving an over-loaded job and becoming self-employed; booking myself into a private clinic for two weeks' complete rest; facing my own physical and sexual abuse as a child.

Social Worker

Finding someone who understands, meeting my own needs as well those of clients; realizing that I was only pretending that I could cope; having a good supervisor.

Registered General Nurse

Having the help of friends who were simply there – available, understanding and accepting; realizing that time would heal; accepting that it is part of me that cannot endure the trauma without some lasting change; gaining insight into what it is all about.

Registered Mental Nurse

Taking time out from work; getting professional help (private counselling); cutting out my heavy drinking; admitting my feelings to friends who were non-judgemental, supportive and understanding; learning to become more assertive; setting aside time for leisure activities; admitting that some of my expectations were impossible or unlikely to be achieved; adapting a philosophy of 'look after myself more'; planning rewards – holidays, meals out.

Social Worker

Pacing myself; cutting my work load; becoming less conscientious (and possibly more effective); making the decision to get another job.

AIDS Worker

Making the decision to leave, to get out of the country for good; putting a thick boundary between work and home.

You, too, can make the necessary changes. If you fear the uncertainty of change, you can take some measures to make some things more certain. If you say: 'I don't know what it would be like living in another area,' visit that area; spend a weekend there. Get the feel of the place. Ask yourself what you want out of a town and check what's available. Note how friendly (or otherwise) shopkeepers and passers-by are when you ask for help. Buy local papers, see what's on and get some idea of the lifestyle of the place.

If you feel that you would be letting people down by changing your commitments, consider what more you could give if you were fit and healthy.

Take your doubts and uncertainties one at a time.

If your aptitudes, personality and abilities do not mesh with the demands of your current profession, this is sad. But it is even more sad to remain. If your expectations have been broken, at least you are in touch with a firmer reality.

Don't attempt to try everything at once. Do what you feel is right for you. Take your time. The aim is to make some limited progress, so that you feel you are beginning to take control. You give yourself hope, you relieve some immediate tensions and you begin to see some movement in your life.

LIFE-EVENT STRESS

If burnout arises from a series of unfortunate events, the way out is to follow some of the earlier guidelines:

- take a break
- plan to reduce your current commitments
- tackle the immediate problem, get professional help if necessary
- develop compensatory interests

If the events were problems you played a part in initiating, look back and see what you could have done differently. You can, at least, learn something from what has happened. You cannot do anything to modify the past – but you can fashion the present and the future.

What if the events were outside your control? That's it. They are over now. Finished. When we have to move on in our lives, some of us still cling to the past. We refuse to accept that things are different. Why? Sometimes it is because the thought of facing a different future immobilizes us. We cannot think straight. Thoughts and feelings flood into our minds. We fight old battles. We retain anger, bitterness and guilt. We may attempt to deny that things are different, like the person who still travels to work although he has been made redundant. We may try to minimize our problems. There may be feelings of depersonalization, where we feel cut off from others. We may feel powerless to tackle what needs to be tackled.

The way forward is to 'own' our feelings, let them work their way through our minds and bodies – and then let go of the past. Yes, there will be regret. There may be a period of bereavement. But this has to be gone through. Our world has changed and we have to change as well. We are where we are. However hard we try to force things, we cannot live the life of five years ago, or live in the nineteenth or twenty-first century. We have the current year in which to live. We need to step out, try things out, learn new skills, form new relationships, check out what suits us and what doesn't. We slowly fashion a new life for ourselves and become integrated with it. We may then be able to look back and find some significance and meaning for what has happened to us.

References

M. Argyle, *The Scientific Study of Human Behaviour* (Methuen, 1957).
R. D. Bailey, *Coping with Stress and Caring* (Blackwell Scientific, 1985.)

R. J. Burke and R. Weir, 'Coping with the stress of managerial occupations', in C. Cooper and R. Payne (eds.), *Current Concerns in Occupational Stress* (Wiley, 1988.)

P. Burnard, 'Beyond burnout', *Nursing Standard*, 5.43, 1991.

K. E. Claus and J. T. Bailey (eds.), *Living with Stress and Promoting Well-being* (C. V. Mosby, 1980.)

R. Evision, 'Self-help in preventing stress build-up', *The Professional Nurse*, March, 1986.

L. M. Garland and C. T. Bush, *Coping Behaviours and Nursing* (Preston, 1982.)

J. Gilmartin, 'Stress in relation to the nurse teacher', unpublished dissertation, 1990.

E. Goffman, *Where the Action Is* (Allen Lane, 1969.)

G. B. Graen, 'Role making processes within complex organizations', in M. D. Dunnette (ed.), *Handbook of Industrial and Organizational Psychology* (Rand McNally, 1971.)

D. Katz and R. Kahn, *The Social Psychology of Organisations*, (Wiley, 1966.)

J. Kechie, 'Opting out of burnout', *Nursing Times*, 87, 1991.

T. M. Kuhlmann, 'Coping with occupational stress among urban bus and tram drivers', *Journal of Occupational Psychology*, 63, 1990.

V. D. Lachman, *Stress Management* (Grove & Stratton, 1983.)

R. Linton, *The Cultural Background of Personality* (Appleton-Century, 1945.)

I. S. Schonfeld, 'Coping with job-related stress: the case of teachers', *Journal of Occupational Psychology*, 63, 1990.

S. Wright et al., 'Coping with stress, the good and the bad', *Nursing Times*, 84.11, 1988.

P. Zimbardo and E. B. Ebbesen, *Management Competencies: Influencing Attitudes and Behaviours*, (Addison-Wesley, 1970.)

4

TACKLING BURNOUT AND STRESS

TECHNIQUES THAT HELP

The way to work through burnout is to find some respite and ease some of the more pressing stressors so that you can take a fundamental look at what you need to do in the long term. If you need to get out of your present work environment and possibly consider a different career path, these are important steps that have to be taken to ensure that your future life is fulfilling and not draining. If you cannot see circumstances improving at work, it is destructive to just wait around hoping that something will happen until you are forced to do something because of a physical or mental collapse. You can initiate steps to remove yourself from these circumstances. Initially, it may be difficult – but it can be done. You will be investing in your future happiness.

It may be that you feel you could do something to improve the conditions under which you work or to increase your skills or learn how to cope in a more efficient and constructive way. Such techniques in themselves have limited value. For example, learning to relax so that the cares of the day are soothed away is a good thing, but to do so and ignore dealing with some of the important causes of your stress (such as work-overload and personality conflict) is not a very effective way to start to take control of your life. What relaxation is likely to do is to lower your tension level, remove some of the adverse physiological effects of stress and make some of the problems you need to tackle less daunting.

THE TECHNIQUES

Relaxation

The instructions may look complicated, but if you take them a few at a time, you will find that you become skilled relatively quickly. You can make a cassette of these suggestions or there is a specially prepared cassette available from the address given in the Useful Addresses chapter of the book.

Find a comfortable place where you can sit down and will not be disturbed. Make sure your back is upright. You can lie down if you wish, but if you are tired you are likely to fall asleep. This is fine if you want to sleep. Certainly, a relaxed half-hour's sleep is beneficial, but by sitting up you are more likely to remain in a comfortable, drowsy state similar to how you feel just before you fall asleep, which is a good way to begin any relaxation session.

You don't have to try hard – this will not help you relax. Just let things happen. Take your time.

Take a slow, deep breath, filling your lungs completely. Hold and slowly breathe out to the count of five: one, two, three, four, five. As you do so, imagine that every part of your body is relaxing, that all tension is flowing out of you. Do this a few more times. You should begin to feel calmer.

Count backwards: five, four, three, two, one; and as you reach 'one', look upwards as if through the top of your head or the top of your eyebrows.

Don't strain your head by bending it upwards – just let your eyes look upwards. Pause.

Count: one, two, three, four, five; and close your eyes as you reach 'five'. Let yourself relax. Pause and slowly let the whole of your body relax. Remain like this for a few moments.

Count: five, four, three, two, one – open your eyes as you did before. Look upwards. Your eyes are likely to ache a little at this stage.

Count: one, two, three, four, five; close your eyes as you reach 'five'. Tell yourself that you are becoming twice as relaxed as you were previously. Just say it to yourself quietly. Imagine all the major parts of your body in turn and visualize them becoming twice as relaxed.

Count: five, four, three, two, one. Open your eyes. Look upwards as you did previously. Pause. Your eyes will feel heavy and you will find it difficult to keep them open. But keep them open a little longer.

Count: one, two, three, four, five; close your eyes. Say to yourself that you are becoming ten times as relaxed as you were previously. Repeat this quietly a few times and then visualize all the parts of your body becoming ten times as relaxed.

Feel how relaxed you are. Now count backwards from 300, that is 299, 298 – and so on. As you do so, imagine that your mind is becoming more and more relaxed with each number you say to yourself. Continue until you feel mentally relaxed and then let the number go . . .

Now imagine that there are three levels of relaxation, each more deep than the one before it. There is level one, level two and level three. Imagine that you are going down to level one. If it helps, see yourself walking down steps until you reach a sign which says 'Level 1'. Pause and then make your way down to level two. If it helps, imagine that you are on an escalator going down gently until you reach the bottom and see a sign saying 'Level 2'. Now imagine that you are floating down to level three until you see a sign saying 'Level 3'.

Finally, imagine that you are in a very beautiful place, a garden perhaps, or a beach you visited on holiday. Feel the warmth of the sun on your face, the gentle breeze floating lightly over your skin. Look at the clear blue sky, let the scent of the flowers drift towards you. Let yourself become part of the scene. Imagine that you notice a very comfortable-looking chair or sofa. Go over to it. Sit down and *notice how deeply relaxed you feel. Now imagine all your worries, stresses and problems are floating away from you and being replaced with calm, peaceful healing. Fill yourself with the feeling.*

When you feel ready to come out of your relaxation, count backwards: five, four, three, two, one – open your eyes, focus on different parts of your room. Then stretch.

The process may seem complicated, but after a few attempts you should be able to master it quite easily. Take your time. Remember you can bring yourself out of your relaxation anytime you like by counting backwards: five, four, three, two, one. Practise coming out a few times.

When you have reached a reasonable level of proficiency in relaxing, try relaxing by counting from 'one' to 'five' and breathing out slowly as you do so. Imagine that you are becoming more and more relaxed as you think of each number. Or you may try imagining that you are in that beautiful place. You can use this method as soon as you start to feel tense.

Becoming More Assertive

Becoming more assertive opens up new and constructive ways of dealing with colleagues and others. It helps reduce stress because you don't feel so trapped when you realize that you have power to make things go your way.

You can respond in one of four ways when you are asked to do something you dislike:

1. You can accept passively.
2. You can respond aggressively.
3. You can agree but try to wreck things in a hidden way.
4. You can act assertively.

Look at some of these situations:

Jane is asked to work late. She has an appointment she doesn't want to miss but she finds herself saying 'Yes'. She is resentful but stays behind. By saying 'Yes,' she is actually training her manager to impose on her in this way. She rewards (technically reinforces) her manager's behaviour.

Tom also stays late but mislays some important information that's going to get his manager into trouble. 'That will teach him', he says to himself.

Joe has a row and storms out.

None of these is very constructive.

Being assertive works on the assumption that your needs are as important as anyone else's; that you have the right to ask for what you want (as do other people); that you have the right to say 'No' without feeling guilty.

To start to become more assertive, start with less threatening situations on which to practise, then move up to more difficult circumstances.

One very important element helps smooth the process of assertiveness: listen. Yes – really listen – to what other people are saying. As mentioned in Chapter 3, let them know you have been listening by responding in a way that shows them you have taken on board what they have said. You present back to them their comments, feelings and ideas:

'So what you are saying, Tom, is that the process is going to work out to be too costly?'

'You seem quite angry about this, Mary.'

To do this you have to attend to what is being said; and your body language can help show that you are doing this. You can reflect the actual words used, the main points, the theme and the feelings. Sometimes it's helpful to reflect discrepancies:

'You say you agree, Bill, but you look so uncertain about it.'

Reflecting does not mean that you are agreeing. It means

that the other person knows that you've heard his or her viewpoint.

After reflecting, you add what you want to say:

'You may feel it is not possible, Sarah, but it's important to me that I get some additional help.'

If you are being criticized and you feel it is justified, accept it and state that you want the session to be a problem-solving one. If you feel it is unjustified, present your case, indicating that you understand what has been said but that you do not agree with it.

Negotiating Skills

Negotiating skills are not just a question of a few clever techniques. They are about how people react in situations of uncertainty, complexity and ambiguity. Both sides try to make sense of what is going on and to ascertain what the other side really wants. There are usually a number of stages: interpretation – where you give your own meaning to what the other person is saying; exploration – where you both examine what the issues are, explore each other's perceptions and where there may be a conflict to be worked through; bid and counterbid; and finally (hopefully) positive decision-making.

In many work situations, power is unevenly balanced in favour of the person superior in the firm's or organization's hierarchy. Usually, however, your manager will wish to retain not just your services but your goodwill as well, and what you may be asking for is likely to make you more motivated and possibly more effective. You need to think out the benefits to the organization. You need to put yourself in your manager's shoes and see things from his or her point of view. In this way, you can anticipate your manager's response and, in turn, your methods of tackling it. You need to consider alternatives and your final fallback position. Do not make hasty decisions in the heat of the moment. You may regret these later.

The way both sides see the negotiations is important, because this colours attitudes to the whole process. Some see it as a game, rather like poker, where intentions are hidden and moves are made to gain an advantage. Another way of perceiving it is as a struggle, with the other side as the enemy and co-operation unlikely, the aim being to win at any cost and by any means. Another way is to see negotiations as a collaborative process in which each side explores how both can get as much as they want without detriment to the other. This means considering alternatives and making sacrifices to gain mutual advantage. But it is important not to ignore contentious issues just to keep harmony.

The best advice is to try the collaborative approach first, unless your manager or organization is almost completely unreasonable. Take risks in asking for what you want, but be willing to explore alternatives. You aim for a 'win-win' situation and not for a victor and vanquished.

Studying Your Job

What Is Being Done? What Are the End Results?

Challenge whether what is produced is really needed. Is it all necessary? What do end-users do with it? What would happen if they never received it? It is amazing how frequently reports and information is provided (sometimes at great cost) that is never used.

The key is to see what can be eliminated.

Why Is it Done at that Time?

Bottlenecks often exist because too many tasks come together at the same time. Could it be done later, earlier, less frequently? Are the cycle and sequence right? Could part of the cycle be eliminated, modified or merged? What are the major hold-ups? Analyse interruptions.

Where Is it Being Done?

Why that place? Could it be done more easily elsewhere? Could it be done locally or centrally, or be combined with a previous stage? What about work being done at home (in working, not leisure time)? Computers, word processors, modems enable people to produce reports at home easily. Sometimes they can be produced in the time it takes to travel to work.

Who Does It?

Why that person? Who else could do it? What skills would best help implement the project? Has the best person been chosen for the task? Perhaps more than one person is needed? Do colleagues who work well together get assigned to collaborative tasks?

How is it Done?

Why that method? How could the process be improved? Could it be simplified? Mechanized? Compressed?

Managing Your Time

Time management can help to reduce stress. First you need to have examined if there are any hidden barriers to reducing your workload. Some people use overload as a defence against facing difficult issues. It can provide a 'reason' for not tackling the heart of a problem, but is not a means of tackling burnout. You need to apply the measures outlined above on studying your job. In most jobs it is possible to find some tasks that can be eliminated altogether, without loss of efficiency, and others that can be improved so that they can be carried out more easily.

To go further, you need to record all your major activities. This provides you with a list of main categories. It might include such items as:

- attending meetings
- writing reports and letters
- travelling
- telephoning
- interviewing

When you have done this, prepare a time diary in which you can record how much time you spend on each activity. Select a suitable recording period, not a time when you are over-busy or very slack. Break the diary into 15-minute intervals. Note what you do during each of these periods of time, for example:

- 9:00 attend briefing meeting
- 9:15 still at meeting
- 9:30 still there
- 10:00 open mail
- 10:15 deal with urgent mail items
- and so on.
- Also note any interruptions.

At the end of the recording period (and it needs to last about two weeks), calculate the percentage of time you spend on each of the main categories, for example:

- meetings – 50 per cent
- writing – 20 per cent

- visiting clients – 30 per cent
- and so on.

Examine your interruptions. One study showed that an average manager was interrupted every eight minutes. This doesn't mean 9:00, 9:08, 9:16, etc. You may go for an hour or more without interruptions and then the interruptions are uninterrupted! Some of us actually encourage these. When someone comes in to visit us, we are always ready to stop what we are doing and listen. In this way we train others to interrupt us. We may welcome the interruptions because they stop us getting on with work we would rather not do. For others, they create the impression of lots of activity. We feel lots of things are happening.

The next step is to take a look at major categories that account for large percentages of your time. Consider how these could be reduced, how you could improve your competencies. Try to get at exactly what is so time-consuming about such activities.

Look back over the last month or so and see whether any of your work overloads could have been avoided. What exactly caused the problems?

You need to establish priorities about what items you have to attend, that is, that are essential, and which are only desirable. Don't condemn procrastination. Use it to put off things that don't matter, but then be sure to get stuck into things that do!

Help others to be brief when they visit you. Summarize what they've said in a few words. Reinforce their behaviour by thanking them for coming straight to the point.

Become more proactive rather than just responding to what happens. Create a momentum.

Don't undertake complex work when you are tired. It will take you longer and you will make more mistakes. If you are a 'morning person', tackle difficult tasks and ones that call upon your creativity then. If you find that you are at your best in the afternoon (this is less usual), do this sort of work after lunch.

If problems are caused by other departments, call a meeting to discuss things.

'Stopping' and Visualization

'Stopping' is a technique to cut negative thoughts from taking over your mind and making you thoroughly depressed. One negative thought usually leads to another and then another – and so on, until you feel absolutely miserable. If you have a poor self-image, you may find yourself reminding yourself that you are no good, and this makes you think of the last time you made a mistake, which reminds you that you are a failure, until finally you feel that life holds nothing for you.

The method is simple. As soon as the first negative thought comes into your mind, say to yourself: 'Stop,' and then add an appropriate, positive affirmation such as: 'I really am OK.'

You may not feel like saying this, but do so, and put some feeling into it. You may need to repeat it regularly throughout the day. Work out positive affirmations that match your needs. Make them reasonably realistic. Don't say: 'I am the best person in the world,' but something like 'I am able to grow in confidence.' As with the other techniques, you have to keep at it and practise.

Visualization is another useful technique. Allow yourself to day-dream positive images. Imagine yourself being able to cope competently, see yourself in your mind as acting confidently. Use your imagination to prepare and build in your mind a positive future.

Shaping New Behaviours

A way of changing the way you respond to threatening

situations is to prepare a hierarchy, starting with the most threatening and working down to the least threatening, for example:

1. The most stressful
2. The second most stressful
3. The third most stressful
4. The second least stressful
5. The least stressful

Take the least stressful (number 5). Imagine yourself in that situation. Capture the atmosphere. Who is there? What are you doing? Note your physical response to the situation. Do your shoulders tighten, do you feel a headache coming on, sick inside your stomach, tightness across the chest? Whatever it is – note the physical sensation. Let the scene float away.

Now start to imagine the scene once again – but this time, as soon as you do so, start to count: one, two, three, four, five. Relax as you breathe out, or imagine your beautiful place.

Practise this a number of times and you will begin to 'pair' the relaxation with one of your problem areas. When you find that the lower order problem no longer bothers you, move (in your imagination) to the next, more stressful situation and repeat the process. You can do so with all levels until you reach the most threatening. Then you need to start to use the technique in real life. Start with less threatening experiences and move up your hierarchy. As soon as you feel your physiological stress trigger, count from one to five and breathe out gently. Imagine that you are relaxing as you do so.

It is no use trying the technique once or twice, you have to keep practising it. By doing so, you will learn to control your negative, stressful emotions.

Gradually you will begin to see what life could be like for you as you move out of situations that have caused you burnout and into a more fruitful future. You will have moved out of your prison. The future will be one created by your own actions. You will have taken responsibility for yourself.

An important buffer to stress is to develop a 'hardy' personality. This consists of:

- believing that you can control things
- being committed to what you want for yourself, your family and in your job
- seeing challenge as an opportunity rather than a threat

You have to start from where you are. You may decide you need professional help to deal with some of your problems. This is one way of using available resources to develop your potential.

Perseverance is necessary. Do not expect everything to change at once. Once you have made a decision, the world does not react immediately. Do not expect radical change if you just dabble half-heartedly with a few techniques. Attempt things – even if you are nervous. Confidence comes from doing things even if you are afraid.

You do not have to be the victim of past experience, class background or your present circumstances. Become the creator of your own future.

References

H. Benson, *The Relaxation Response* (Avon, 1975.)

W. C. Coe, *Hypnosis and Suggestion in Behavioural Change: Helping People to Change* (Pergamon, 1980.)

D. C. Rimm, 'Thought stopping and covert assertion in the treatment of phobias', *Journal of Clinical Psychology*, 41, 1973.

5

LOOKING DEEPER

THE HIDDEN CAUSES OF STRESS AND BURNOUT

You've seen that burnout results from chronic stress, when you have continued to battle on until your body and mind shout for help; when you feel you have little energy left to tackle daily problems and when, despite everything you do, you seem to achieve little.

If stress has culminated in burnout for you and you have already taken some of the immediate remedial actions suggested, you will have given yourself some breathing space. You may have decided to remove yourself from situations that cause your difficulties. Or you may sense that you are near burnout, but not yet at that stage. In either case, you may find it helpful to take a deeper look at yourself to see what is behind the stress in your life.

PERSONAL CONSTRUCT PSYCHOLOGY

First you need to know a little about the philosophy behind this chapter. It is based on the ideas and some of the techniques of Personal Construct Psychology (PCP). PCP is about how we perceive (or construe) our world. From our massive and complex construct system, we act and feel as we do about the things that confront us daily. We enter the future by looking backwards. As the future turns into the present, our past experiences guide us about what to do. This is the purpose of our construct system: to enable us to anticipate the future and to deal with it.

Of course, it is impossible to grasp ultimate reality. To live, we have to parcel parts of the world that concern us into manageable segments and define them. By doing this, we impose some of our own meanings on reality as we decide what segments we choose to absorb and how to define them. We break things up this way because it is convenient. It makes things manageable.

A chemist defines reality in terms of chemical structures, a sociologist in the form of social institutions and structures, a poet in yet another way. Some cultures do not recognize time, and in their languages there are no tenses; others have no nouns – everything is a verb (an action).

This is how the same 'realities' can be construed quite differently. Even in the same culture or family – we may only *think* we see everything the same way. It is not so much a question of right and wrong but of usefulness. Sometimes the way we see our world is not all that useful; for example, we may feel that the world is a pretty dangerous place to live in most of the time. No doubt it is, some of the time. But if we feel most aspects of living are unsafe, we act defensively most of the time. We use up a lot of our energy and our resources to buy 'security'. By so doing, we are likely to miss many other aspects of a potentially interesting life.

If you take a group of people working in an organization and ask them to describe what it is like, you get some agreement – but also many differences of opinion. ' A place of opportunity,' says one; 'They exploit you here,' says another. Many things, people, events and circumstances are open to different interpretations. By viewing situations from other viewpoints, we may find more constructive ways of dealing with them. This does not mean that there are no physical and social realities which provide finite boundaries. What it does mean is that, more frequently than we realize, we are trapped by our understanding of events or our belief about what we can do about them.

Ask a pessimist to describe his visit to a shopping centre. He reports on 'weary people, trudging around during a cold, dull day, bombarded with the intrusive noise of traffic, in the half-empty shops and the general drabness'. How does the optimist see the same scene? He notes 'the bustle of activity, the way people chat and laugh together and how the shops are half full of people'. Both are validating their view of the world. We look for evidence to support what we believe.

We are subjected to a mass of stimuli – far too much for us to process, so we have to be selective. And we select to fit our expectations.

This understanding helps us realize that there may be alternative ways of seeing things, and this can open up fresh opportunities. If we believe that it is our duty to stay in an unfulfilling job, then there we stay. If we feel that we cannot do anything to improve things, then we don't bother. Our view of our problem becomes a self-fulfilling prophecy. Even if we know something doesn't work, we sometimes go on repeating the same ineffective behaviour – because that's what we always do.

In some ways, it is threatening to think we could challenge our precious assumptions about things; but it is also liberating and creative. We can explore other meanings and see where they would lead us. If we are not certain about things, we can hold tentative beliefs and check them out, amending or confirming our views. This process provides us with opportunities.

We don't just respond to stimuli as the behaviourists would suggest, we respond to meanings and we can (within limits) reconstrue these meanings.

OUR CONSTRUCT SYSTEM —
OUR WAY OF VIEWING OUR WORLD

We are part of a number of complex social networks, ranging from small family units to large institutions. These networks help define who we are. In part, this is because people respond to us because of the way we present ourselves to them. If I think people don't like me, I act as if they dislike me. I don't smile. I don't put much effort into greeting them. I appear defensive. From what I say, how I act and my non-verbal communication, my messages are pretty clear. Soon people stop being friendly to me. I am now disliked and I am able to feel that I was right all along.

Sometimes, what happens is that others try to 'altercast' you, they attempt to push you into the roles they want you to play; where, for example, you are placed in an inferior position to them. If you know what they are doing, you do not have to accept it.

If you believe that you are trapped, you act as if there is no way out. You don't bother to try and escape. But if you start to examine alternative meanings for the situation you are in, you might find there are possibilities that you can explore.

Why We Stay As We Are

If all this is so, why then do we continue with inappropriate behaviours? Frequently, because of the advantages in doing so. If you are stuck in an unsatisfactory job, at least you know where you are. It is safer than moving out. You limit your risks and avoid possible failure. Becoming proactive, rather than just responding to what turns up, takes initiative and causes uncertainty, and this can be threatening. Facing up to such threats, learning how to deal with them and accepting whatever discomfort is involved, puts us more in touch with constructive ways of living. We are no longer stuck. We can get on with life.

Our Constructs – A Way into Meaning

Understanding something of our construct system is the start of our exploration. It helps pin-point the meanings behind problems. Construct systems consist of a complex, interrelated network of subsystems and individual constructs. Individual constructs may be thought of as units of perception. These units are not static entities – but processes. We modify them and the way they are related to other constructs in the light of new experiences. A new situation may resemble an old one but with variations. If we retain our childhood way of seeing things, we are unable to tackle many of our adult responsibilities. Most of us discard old ideas that do not fit, but a few hang on to beliefs about the world that are out of touch with the new realities that face us. We might attempt to live by outmoded parental dictats: 'Don't take risks,' 'Behave yourself, fun is wrong,' 'Be perfect,' and so on. We may even try to force the world to see things our way (this is the definition of hostility in PCP terms).

We share some of our constructs with others (commonality). Other constructs are understood, but not shared, by others (sociality), and a few are unique to ourselves (individuality).

As mentioned in Chapter 3, constructs are bipolar; for example:

- hate<->love
- depression<->happiness
- tight<->loose

Note how the opposites may not be antonyms in a strict

sense. Other people might have revealed their constructs by setting forth these opposite pairs:

- indifference<->love
- sadness<->happiness
- tight<->free

Constructs, as already mentioned, are linked to other constructs into subsystems, which are related to even larger systems. Some constructs are subordinate to other, superordinate ones. We may be fully aware of our constructs or they may exist at lower levels of consciousness.

Exploring Constructs

Constructs can be studied in many ways. You can start to understand something about how you construe your world by talking or writing about it. You select an area you want to study and limit your enquiries to that area. Here we are concerned with stress and burnout.

To assist in this process, 'elements' are selected from within a given area. Elements are persons, events, situations or anything connected with the domain under review.

For example, to study stress, you might include events such as:

- the last time you can remember when you felt stressed at work
- a time when you were with a group and felt stressed

There is a specialized technique known as a 'repertory grid' which helps reveal your constructs by using the elements selected.

Most stress research has concentrated on:

- Events that cause stress
- The physiological aspects of stress
- The type of personalities more prone to stress
- Coping strategies

This work has value, but it can miss a very important point. We don't just respond to situations in themselves – but to the meanings these situations hold for us.

WHAT HAPPENS WHEN WE'RE STRESSED?

When we are stressed the sympathetic part of our autonomic nervous system is activated; adrenalin is released, our heart rate increases, blood-pressure rises, breathing quickens, and blood is redirected to the brain, heart and muscles. Cortisol is released – this thickens the blood so it clots more easily. Hydrochloric acid is increased. Digestion is slowed. There are changes in metabolism. The liver increases the levels of glucose (sugar) in the blood. When the stressful event is over, your body releases noradrenalin. You begin to feel calm.

Sudden surges in blood-pressure are unhealthy and noradrenalin released daily, week after week for a number of years, physically harms the arteries in the heart. Other long-term effects of stress include: an impaired immune system – the ability to fight off germs is less efficient and illness becomes more frequent; the endorphine release system is reduced – pain is felt more intensely.

It is the meaning we have about an event that sets in motion the physiological processes outlined above. For example, one person finds public speaking terrifying because he feels he is on trial, while another finds it exciting because she likes the challenge of sharing her ideas with people. Some dislike flying, others find it fun. Some see their annual work assessment as a trial, others as a co-operative venture to iron out problems, increase work satisfaction and improve efficiency.

The Personal Construct approach to stress is used to uncover meanings so that strategies can be evolved which deal with the heart of our specific problems and not with generalities.

WORKING WITH STRESS

Here's a way of finding the hidden meanings behind your stress. It uses elements connected with stress and repertory grid techniques to analyse and explore these meanings. Read the process through quickly to get the feel of what it is about. Then work through the exercises. Take your time. You don't have to do the lot in one session. Remember, there are no right or wrong answers, only your answers.

Step One

Think of the last time you were stressed. You may want to concentrate on your work environment, or take a wider scope. Just trust yourself to accept whatever comes into your mind.

Spend some time thinking about the event. Where were you? Recapture the environment, the people, the colours, the whole situation. What did you do? What would you have liked to have done?

You're likely to find that your feelings are beginning to mimic how you felt at the time. You can see how even thinking about a stressful situation initiates physiological responses.

Give this event a name. Something that you can recall it by. Write the name down on a piece of paper.

Step Two

Think of a good event in your life. If your first choice is limited to your working life, use work again for your second selection. A time when you felt happy. Make it something specific. Again recall all you can of the event. Recapture it fully in your mind. Dwell on it for a moment. Again give it a name to remember it by and write that name down on a piece of paper.

You can see that by thinking about events, you begin to experience some of the feelings associated with them at the time. Your mind can truly affect your body.

An additional point here is that when you dwell on a negative situation, going over and over it in your mind, you affect yourself physiologically. Think of an embarrassing situation and you may find your face gets hot.

Step Three

Think of another stressful event in your life (again about work if your previous choices have been in this area). This time, do not dwell on it. Write down a suitable name for it on a piece of paper.

Step Four

You now have three events:

1. stressful
2. pleasant (not stressful)
3. stressful

Ask yourself what quality the two stressful events share. You may find this difficult, or something may come flooding into your mind. Avoid anything superficial – such as both happened on a Friday. Look for a quality. Here are some examples (but do stay with your own, they are so much more important for you):

- 'I felt out of control'
- 'I felt a failure'
- 'I couldn't express the anger I felt'
- 'I felt totally overwhelmed'

You now need to think of opposites to what you've written down. Note, These are to be *your* opposites, not the ones you might find in a dictionary. As mentioned earlier, constructs have bipolar opposites. The first concept that came into your mind is called the 'emergent' pole. By thinking of its opposite, you begin to understand something of the individual meaning you gave it.

Here are some examples:

- 'I felt out of control'<->'I knew I could handle it'
- 'I felt a failure'<->'I was full of confidence'
- 'I couldn't express the anger I felt'<->'I was able to express exactly how I felt, without guilt'
- 'I felt totally overwhelmed'<->'I felt stimulatingly challenged'

Take a look at events numbered 1 and 3 again. Are there any other qualities they share? If so, do the same exercise again by writing down the quality and its opposite.

Look separately at event number 1. Are there any qualities which it has, which the other two do *not* share? If so, write them down with their opposites.

You may have only one or you may have elicited four or more *constructs* (definitions) from the first set of three *elements* (stressful events, people, or situations – technically called triads).

Figure 6: Repertory Grid Form

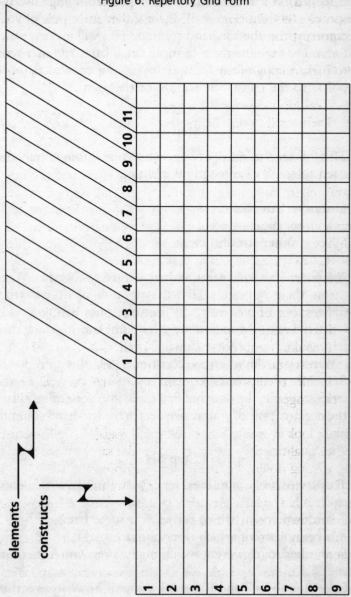

To help you keep track of what you are doing, use the special grid form (Figure 6). Place the negative pole of your constructs on the left-hand column. This will make it easier for you to examine them in more detail later. You may wish to make a copy of the form. Transfer your constructs (both poles) to the constructs section of this form.

Step Five

This follows the same pattern as steps one through four. You need to think of three more events:

4. another stressful event
5. another pleasant event
6. yet another stressful event

Ask yourself in what way numbers 4 and 6 go together. Write down their opposites. Try to get a different construct (description of how you felt) from the ones you've already written down. If you find more than one way in which they go together, write these down as well.

Write your new stress constructs on the grid form. Remember constructs contain opposites as well as the emergent pole, the one that first came into your mind. Place the negative pole of your constructs in the left-hand column.

Step Six

This consists of a similar exercise, with three new elements:

7. a routine event which causes you some stress
8. a routine event which does not stress you
9. another routine event which might stress you sometimes

Select numbers 7 and 9 and ask yourself in what ways they

are alike. Now choose words to describe their opposites. Write them on the form.

Step Seven

You can now look for similarities in the following combinations:

3, 2 and 4
6, 5 and 7
1, 8 and 9

Don't worry if you can't find qualities to describe them all. Or you may, of course, find more than one for each combination. If you find that the same constructs begin to repeat themselves, it is likely that you have established all your constructs related to stress and the exercise is complete.

Figure 7 is an example of a completed form. Along the top are the elements and down the side are the constructs. Remember, your examples may be quite different.

Step Eight

Now add two new elements to your form:

• 'self now'
• 'self like to be'

Step Nine

What you now do is to grade each of your constructs against each element. Use a scale of:

1 2 3 4 5

The left-hand (negative) side of the construct represents 1. The right-hand side represents 5. The other figures (2, 3 and 4) are intermediate ratings.

If your first construct is: no control<->in control, and

Figure 7: Grid Form with Constructs and Elements

elements

constructs

	1	2	3	4	5	6	7	8	9	10	11
		sales meeting	customer action	resource planning	evaluation project	external meeting	conflict	word processing	letters	finding 'lost' files	

1 no control – in control
2 time pressure – no deadlines
3 depression – challenge
4 failure – success
5 feeling guilty – feeling free
6 don't know what to expect – clear
7 insecure – secure
8 no time to think – time enough
9 waste of time – useful

Figure 8: Completed Grid Form with Self Now/Like to Be

elements

constructs

	sales meeting	customer action	resource planning	evaluation project	external meeting	conflict	word processing	letters	finding 'lost' files	self now	self I'd like to be
	1	**2**	**3**	**4**	**5**	**6**	**7**	**8**	**9**	**10 11**	
1 no control – in control											
2 time pressure – no deadlines											
3 depression – challenge											
4 failure – success											
5 feeling guilty – feeling free											
6 don't know what to expect – clear											
7 insecure – secure											
8 no time to think – time enough											
9 waste of time – useful											

your first element was: sales meeting, ask yourself whether you felt in control at that meeting. If you answer 'yes', rate it 5; if you felt partly in control, rate it 4; if you were not really either, rate it 3, if you did not have too much control, rate it 2, and if you felt you had no control, rate it 1. Figure 9 shows a rated grid form.

In the example you can see that sales meeting is graded 2 for no control<->in control; 3 for time pressure<->no deadlines; 3 for depression<->challenge; 1 for failure<->success – and so on.

Rate 'self now' and 'self like to be' for each of the constructs.

You do this by saying how, generally, as far as that particular construct is concerned, you feel currently in your life. Then you do it for how you'd like to be. Most of your 'like to be' entries will probably be rated fairly high – a 4 or 5, for instance.

Step Ten

Look at the differences between 'self now' and 'self like to be'. This quantifies the stress in your life. Look at where the difference is greatest. This is where stress is most severe.

A simple way of calculating the degree of satisfaction or dissatisfaction between 'self now' and 'self like to be' is to total the differences between the two figures, as shown in Table 3:

Table 3

Constructs	Self now	Self like to be
1 no control<->in control	2	5
2 time pressure<->no deadlines	1	5
3 depression<->challenge	1	5

Figure 9: Rated Grid Form

Elements:
1 sales meeting
2 customer action
3 resource planning
4 evaluation project
5 external meeting
6 conflict
7 word processing
8 letters
9 finding 'lost' files
10 self now
11 self I'd like to be

Constructs	1	2	3	4	5	6	7	8	9	10	11
1 no control – in control	2	4	1	1	4	1	2	4	1	2	5
2 time pressure – no deadlines	3	4	2	3	4	1	4	3	2	1	5
3 depression – challenge	3	5	2	2	5	1	4	4	3	1	5
4 failure – success	1	5	2	2	3	1	2	5	1	1	4
5 feeling guilty – feeling free	1	4	2	1	4	1	3	3	2	3	4
6 don't know what to expect – clear	1	5	1	2	4	2	3	3	3	2	4
7 insecure – secure	3	4	2	1	5	1	3	4	3	2	4
8 no time to think – time enough	2	5	2	2	5	3	2	5	2	1	5
9 waste of time – useful	1	5	1	1	4	3	2	1	2	2	5

| 4 | failure<->success | 1 | 4 |
| 5 | feeling guilty<->feeling free | 3 | 4 |

The difference between the two columns is:

Construct	Difference
1	3
2	4
3	4
4	3
5	1
total difference	**15**

Another, more powerful way of measuring your satisfaction/dissatisfaction is to calculate a statistical correlation between them. A correlation provides a range of between −1.0 and +1.0. +1.0 means complete satisfaction (there is no difference between 'self now' and 'self like to be'). This is rare, and in fact, not so positive, as it leaves nothing to strive for. A correlation of 0.0 means that you are not getting what you want out of the aspect of your life that you are studying. If you are unfortunate enough to have −1.0, this means that not only are you not getting what you want, but you are getting very much of what you *don't* want. Usually people have a correlation between +.2 and +.8.

When you've done your calculation (simple difference or correlation), you'll be able to use it to measure your progress. When you do a stress grid again later, you can compare your new total with the old one.

In the example above, the main difficulties are with constructs 2 (time pressure) and 3 (depression).

Step Eleven

There is another important aspect that will help you concentrate your efforts where they will bring more powerful results: the way in which your constructs are related to each other.

To achieve this, you need to compare the pattern of gradings in each row with that of every other row.

To start your comparison, compare row 1 with row 2, then with row 3, then row 4, then row 5 and so on. You can do this either at a glance or by writing out the first row on a narrow strip of paper and comparing it against each of the other rows, moving downward so that you can see whether it is similar to the other rows.

If there are just a few differences in the grades you gave each element/bipolar constructs triad, count the rows as similar.

Repeat the process by comparing row 2 with row 3, then 4, then 5 – and so on.

Next, repeat by comparing row 3 with row 4, then row 5, and so on.

Continue with the remaining rows.

Note the rows which link together (because you have graded them similarly).

You may find that all the rows are similar. You may find that all are different. Most likely, you will find a mixture.

Draw the way your constructs link, using a circle to indicate each construct. Figure 10 provides some examples.

What you have just done is important. If you find that many of your constructs are linked, this suggests that a more powerful construct is 'controlling' them. Generally, the greater the degree of integration the more intense the stress. Someone whose life is more compartmentalized does not let one part of his or her life intrude on other parts.

As you work through the exercise, you may find it useful to pause and consider the implications of one construct.

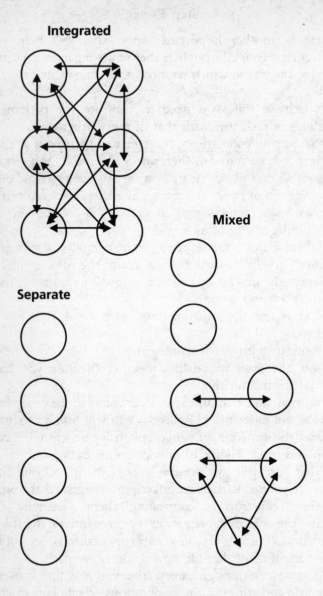

Figure 10: The Way Constructs Can Be Linked

Here is a construct from a 25-year-old engineer:

- difficult planning problems<->total chaos

The 'positive' pole of the construct is: 'total chaos'. What this was all about was that with 'total chaos' all responsibilities were given up and our engineer felt he didn't have to bother. If there were just difficult planning problems, he retained responsibility. Having responsibility made him feel stressed. You might be able to sense the trap he was in. His escape route from stress was 'total chaos', which released him from responsibility. But this made it difficult for him to keep his job.

Let's look at another construct that frequently emerges in studies of stress, this time from an administrator:

- not overloaded<->overloaded

Here the 'positive' pole is, surprisingly, 'overloaded'. The reason for this was that as long as our administrator felt she was overloaded, she did not have to face important issues. She could hide behind a mass of work, receive some sympathy for her efforts and everyone would understand that she just didn't have time to look at longer-term problems.

The usual response to 'overload' is to cut the quantity, variety and complexity of work. But it would not have helped in this case.

Here are another two constructs, this time from a 30-year-old personnel officer:

- depression<->challenge
- fear of failure<->success

This showed an impossible life. Without challenge there was depression. But challenge involves risk, risk includes the possibility of failure, and fear of failure was one of her greatest dreads. So she had the choice of sticking with non-challenging work and feeling depressed or experiencing one of her greatest fears. In practice, she started to take risks to release her from her depression and then to retreat when she sensed a possibility of failure.

How did she eventually deal with this? She explored what she meant by failure, by tracing back the development of her construct throughout her earlier life. As a child, she had been made to feel that she could never win. When she did well in school subjects, her parents never praised her, only pointed out that she should have done better still. She began to free herself from this idea and to break down the blanket concept of 'failure' into those aspects that were her fault and those outside her control.

Those that were her fault she then divided into those that mattered and those that didn't. Those that mattered were further subdivided into errors of detail and errors of principle. She examined her errors of principle to see what patterns emerged and to decide where training would assist her. She looked at her errors of detail to see in what circumstances they had occurred. They were often at the end of the day when she rushed to get things out so that she could go home without a large pending tray. Her method of reducing this was to pace herself better and to leave some things until the next day.

Another example is from an electronics engineer. Here is one of his constructs:

• telling others about unpopular decisions<–>being liked

His main problem was that he had to inform his staff about things they did not welcome and he didn't like upsetting people. He wanted to get them to do things they disagreed with, without them feeling angry with him. But it is natural that people feel angry when they are asked to do things they dislike. What he had to do was to see his hurt at how he felt when they responded to his requests as a measure of his sensitivity. He had to 'own' his hurt. Although it felt strange, it did free him from considerable pressure.

Another example is that of a manager who was uncertain about what she was supposed to do. Ambiguity is a common cause of stress in business organizations.

- role ambiguous<->clear about role

In elaborating this further, it appeared that she had fought hard to oppose any rational means to clear up her ambiguity. What was happening was that she wanted to hold on to her 'ambiguity'. Underneath it all, she sensed what she was supposed to do and this was threatening. So it was safer to let things remain unclear and be able to complain that nobody really told her what was expected. She moved out of her trap by facing up to what was threatening her.

These examples show how exploring constructs can lead to insight and ways of opening up new possibilities by facing the underlying issues.

Does this mean that an organization should only work at the level of the individual? The answer is no. There will be some constructs that are common and that can be tackled more efficiently at an organizational level. It also means that we should beware of a simplistic approach which ignores the individual factors.

Even at an organizational level, it is important to realize that the mixtures of stress constructs will differ from organization to organization, and that applying a general purpose questionnaire may miss some important points. Figures 11–13 offer some examples of stress constructs in different occupations:

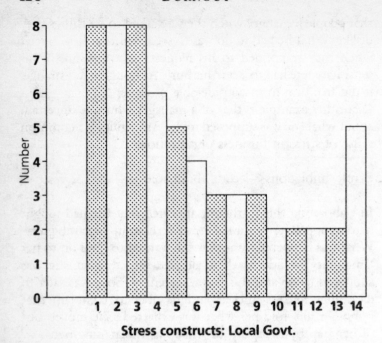

Stress constructs: Local Govt.

1 Overload
2 Not being able to achieve objectives
3 Lack of control
4 My priorities upset by others
5 Time wasted on trivia
6 Work too challenging
7 Lack of help and concern
8 Feeling responsible for others
9 Communications problems
10 Work too difficult for me
11 Not being allowed to use my initiative
12 Lack of confidence
13 Lack of competence
14 Miscellaneous

Figure 11: Stress Constructs/Local Government

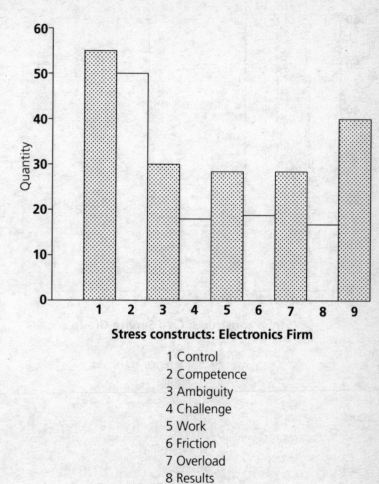

Stress constructs: Electronics Firm

1 Control
2 Competence
3 Ambiguity
4 Challenge
5 Work
6 Friction
7 Overload
8 Results
9 Miscellaneous

Figure 12: Stress Constructs/Electronics Firm

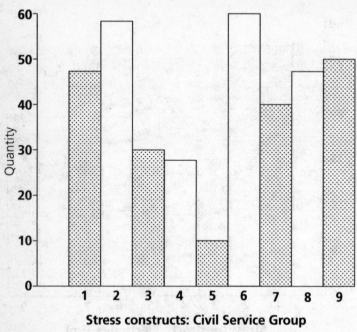

Stress constructs: Civil Service Group

1 Control
2 Competence
3 Ambiguity
4 Challenge
5 Work
6 Friction
7 Overload
8 Results
9 Miscellaneous

Figure 13: Stress Constructs/Civil Service Group

CHANGING YOUR CONSTRUCTS

Work Overload

Work overload is presented as a common cause of stress. One way to tackle it is to examine what you do and how you do it, to see what tasks could be reduced, eliminated or done with less effort. The techniques connected with work study provide a useful framework for this type of research. It is outlined in Chapter 4.

Problems With Roles

Role Conflict

Role conflict takes many forms: being torn between different demands which are difficult to reconcile; feeling responsible to your management team, your staff and your personal belief system; having to work for more than one boss or department, each seeing you with different roles to meet their needs.

There are no easy answers. There is no straight-cut moral rule book to which you can refer. What you can do is to make your difficulties clear, and negotiate. First put yourself in the other person's shoes and see things from his or her point of view. Try to get a meeting of all involved, and present how you see *their* problems and expectations. Check out that your perceptions are correct. Then present your ideas and ask for solutions. Try to build in actions for when things don't work out . . . 'and what shall we do if it doesn't work?'

Some of us try to side-step the conflict that such a meeting might generate. We retain the problem because we aim for harmony – so the tensions remain underground; simmering and poisoning us inside. And the organization is not as efficient as it could be.

If you do try to negotiate, you need to be clear about your bottom line. You may not win everything. Sometimes you will. Other times you will get nothing. Most of the time you should reach a workable compromise. Do not make threats that you do not intend to keep.

As you saw with some of the burnout stories earlier, sometimes the only way out is to leave the organization. If you do this, take your time over it. Leave at a time convenient to you. Do not walk out in anger. If at all possible, do not leave until you've found another job – even if it is only a temporary one.

Role Ambiguity

We've already looked at this briefly. It differs from role conflict. Role ambiguity is being unclear about what's expected of you.

Ambiguity in a new job is to be expected. But for some – uncertainty lingers. If your objectives are unclear, your authority vague and all you know is that your are responsible for results as well as for mistakes, you can try defining your objectives, authority and responsibilities. Present them in writing to your boss. Ask for a meeting to discuss them. Send a written note about amendments. If you do not get anywhere, you can send a note stating that you are going to work within the boundaries mentioned in your earlier note, unless told otherwise.

Here's a grid which explores some of the issues connected with roles. Work through it as you did with the previous exercises.

The elements are:

1. me, now, as a person
2. me as I would like to be

3. me as I expect to become
4. me as my clients expect to see me
5. me as my staff expect me to be
6. me as management expect me to be
7. me as my professional association expects me to be
8. me as I feel society expects me to be
9. me as the inadequate . . .(executive, nurse, doctor, lawyer, manager, etc.)

Select various combinations:
1 2 3
4 5 6
7 8 9
1 4 7
2 5 8
3 6 9
1 5 9
2 3 4
6 7 8

You need not continue through all the possible combinations if you find that the constructs are becoming repetitive.

Here are some examples of what might come out:

- cut corners<->professional service
- only here for the money<->competent
- bewildered<->should know all the answers
- inadequate<->resourceful
- needing support<->giving support
- playing it safe<->being creative
- static<->moving forward

Rate them as you did previously, but this time, look for patterns between the columns, not just from row to row. This will show the relationship between 'self now' and the 'self you would like to be' for each of the constructs, as well as a total figure. How far away are you from that 'self that you'd like to be'? Look at 'self now' and 'self you expect to become'. Is there much of a difference? This measures your optimism.

Look at the differences between how your managers expect you to be and what your staff expect from you. What similarities and differences emerge?

If you want to measure these differences more precisely, calculate the correlation. But even the raw differences will provide you with sufficient information about where your problems lie.

By looking at the relationships between the rows, you can find which constructs are linked to which other ones. You might, taking the example given above, find that moving forward, being creative and being competent are all linked. A computer analysis might indicate that 'being creative' is the main component. This means that to move forward and to become competent are tied up with using your creativity more.

The exercise pin-points some of your problems and the insight this brings will suggest ways forward. You might also get other members of your department to work through a similar exercise and then discuss what comes out. You are likely to find that other staff face problems similar to yours. If so – you could work out joint ways of tackling things.

Behind all stress is tension. A way to reduce tension is to get more balance in your life and to pace yourself better. Relaxation is also a great help, and techniques for relaxing are discussed in Chapter 4. But you need to tackle other matters as well. Otherwise your problems remain – you just feel less tense about them.

Self-Image

Many people who suffer burnout have low self-esteem. Inside, they feel they are no good. They look upon themselves as failures. They notice the things that go wrong for them, ignoring what they do well. They dwell only on their inadequacies.

You'll find that as you begin to take some control over your life and things start to improve, there will be times when you feel more optimistic. You are likely, however, not to dare to accept that life is beginning to change for the better. Having a grim life is a sort of insurance policy. You feel that you will never be let down. Likewise, with yourself – if you feel you don't amount to much, you have a wonderful excuse for not bothering.

Try living as an optimist for a week. See what it feels like. Every time you think of something negative, fill your mind with positive thoughts. Value yourself as a person. All you have to be, in order to be OK, is to be yourself and that's enough. From time to time, reward yourself for the progress you make.

Keep things in perspective. If you make a mistake – don't 'catastrophize'. It is one mistake. It probably doesn't matter. Programme yourself for success by acting as if you are successful; telling yourself that you are successful and pushing negative ideas out of your mind. Try this for a week. Really try it – and see what happens.

Create options for yourself. There are choices available to you if you go out and create them. If you wait for good things to happen, you may have to wait a long time. If you create a dozen possibilities – some of them will succeed.

Relationships

If most of the stress in your life is about your relationship with your partner, working through the next exercise could help clear a pathway to better understanding. Both partners need to work through the grid separately and then to compare results openly.

Read through the section first to get an idea of what's involved and then return to work on it in more detail.

Prepare your own grid form. Along the top line place the elements (given below). Write the constructs in the column on the left-hand side, as you have done with previous grids.

Here are the elements:

1. yourself now
2. yourself as you used to be when you first got to know your partner
3. yourself as a child (accept whatever age comes into mind)
4. yourself as you would like to be
5. yourself as you expect to become
6. your partner now
7. your partner when you first met
8. your partner as you would like him or her to become
9. your partner as you expect him or her to become

Work through these combinations:

1 2 3
1 2 4
1 4 5
6 7 8
6 8 9
1 6 8
2 6 8

Use the same method outlined previously. Ask yourself which two elements (within each of your combinations of three) go together. Write the quality they share and its opposite (to make up a complete construct) on the grid form. Place the negative pole on the left-hand side and the positive pole on the right-hand side. (See Figures 14 and 15 for examples). Then see whether you can get additional constructs out of each combination.

Add these constructs to your list (unless you have already elicited them):

- What I like least about my partner
- What I like most about my partner
- What I like least about myself
- What I like most about myself

Ask yourself – what is the opposite pole for each of these qualities? For example, if the quality you like most in yourself is 'honesty', your opposite might be: 'manipulates people'.

What opposite poles do is define the construct more clearly. In the example just given, 'honesty' seems to be more connected with dealing with people than with stealing things.

Rate each construct against each element as you have done previously. Use a scale of 1 to 5.

The columns compare like this:

1 and 2 show how you have changed since the relationship started.

6 and 7 show how you perceive your partner has changed during the same period.

1 and 4 show how close (or otherwise) you are to being the sort of person you would like to be.

6 and 8 show how close (or otherwise) your partner is to where you would like him or her to be.

1 and 5, 6 and 9 indicate the degree of optimism you have about such changes becoming realities.

1 and 6 compare you with your perception of your partner.

You can also see how different you are from when you were a child. What traits still remain? Is your ideal self near to that of the child?

Figure 14: John's Grid

Elements:
1 myself now
2 myself when we first met
3 myself as a child
4 as I'd like to be
5 as I expect to become
6 Joan now
7 Joan when we first met
8 as I'd like her to be
9 as I expect her to become

constructs	1	2	3	4	5	6	7	8	9	10	11
1 trapped – feeling free	1	5	2	1	1	1	4	4	1		
2 drifting apart – being together	1	5	3	3	1	1	5	5	1		
3 disillusioned – optimistic	2	4	4	4	1	1	3	4	1		
4 bitter – close	1	5	2	5	2	1	5	1	1		
5 irritable – soft	1	4	3	5	1	3	4	5	5		
6 angry – loving	1	5	3	5	1	1	5	5	2		
7 in a rut – sense of excitement	2	5	5	5	3	2	4	5	1		
8 cut off – feel welcome	1	5	3	5	1	1	5	5	3		
9 weak – tough	3	3	4	4	4	5	4	2	5		

Figure 15: Joan's Grid

constructs \ elements	1 myself now	2 myself when we first met	3 myself as a child	4 as I'd like to be	5 as I expect to become	6 John now	7 John when we first met	8 as I'd like him to be	9 as I expect him to become	10	11
1 angry – full of joy	1	5	3	4	1	4	4	2			
2 weak – assertive	4	4	5	4	1	2	3	4			
3 bitter – calm	1	3	3	3	1	3	4	2			
4 boring – fun to be with	3	4	3	5	2	5	4	3			
5 out of my life – in my life	3	3	3	4	1	5	5	3			
6 pessimistic – optimistic	1	5	3	2	1	5	5	3			
7 unable to share – open	1	4	4	3	1	5	5	4			
8 dishonest – honest	4	4	4	3	4	5	4	5			
9 feeling deprived – feeling fulfilled	1	1	3	4	2	4	5	3			

Now exchange grids. Work openly through the differences and similarities. Explore feelings and expectations.

As we can see from John's (Figure 14), he sees himself very differently from the person he was when he first met Joan (the correlation is −.76). His grid shows that he feels trapped, that he is drifting apart from Joan. He is disillusioned with life but not totally so. He is bitter, finds himself much more irritable – and very angry. He feels he is in a rut and cut off from Joan.

He perceives Joan has changed as much as he has, except that she is not so irritable and she remains fairly tough (the correlation is only −.3, much less than for John. But you need to note that, statistically, a correlation of −.3 is not .46 less than −.76).

John is pessimistic about how things will change, either in himself or with Joan.

Grids can be compared. What constructs are similar? Each provides a picture of how the partners see one another and what is important to them. They can ponder over how each felt when they first met and what has happened to cause them to drift apart. John felt freedom, togetherness, optimism, closeness, loving, a sense of excitement. He felt that Joan welcomed him into her life. He now thinks of Joan as tough, much tougher than he is, and he wants a 'softer' person.

John had been under considerable stress, near the burnout stage. Not all of it was connected with his relationship with Joan – but much of it was. His main symptom was fatigue, and he cut himself off from Joan. He wanted Joan to look after him, but she didn't want to be a caretaker-wife.

How does Joan see things? Her grid shows that she also is quite different from the time when she first met John. But not as different as John sees himself to be (his correlation for 'self now' and 'when we first met' is −.76, hers is .1). Joan sees herself as remaining 'assertive'. This is likely to be the same construct that John calls 'tough'. He would like her to be less tough. Joan also wishes to be less 'assertive', but not to the same degree as John. John sees her as the dominant partner.

Joan feels angry, bitter, pessimistic, deprived and unable to share herself with John – a fairly depressing picture. Joan does expect some improvement but – like John – not much. She expects to become less angry, more calm, slightly more optimistic, more open and less deprived, but not so much so that there is a really positive picture. Her limited optimism may not be connected with their future together but with a life apart from John.

Joan grades a construct which she calls 'out of my life' as 3 for when she first met John and as 1 for what she expects him to become – in other words she expects him to be even more outside her life in the future. Even in the early days, for some reason, Joan held herself back from John. This and her 'assertive' characteristic compared with John's 'weakness' didn't matter in their early days together. Life was fresh and new for them. They anticipated a future of happiness. Now with little in their lives together, this may matter much more.

A computer analysis of John's grid suggests that the principal component for him is: 'cut off<–>feel welcome'. Nearly everything else is related to this. To be excluded from Joan's life hurts John deeply. It is not that Joan does this to hurt him. She sees the world differently. It is that John's needs are different from hers and she doesn't realize this. In John's case this is likely to be the major source of his bitterness, irritability and anger. Joan, on the other hand, wants some distance and space in her life. What John calls closeness, Joan sees as an intrusion.

The main construct in Joan's grid is: 'boring<–>fun'. It looks as if Joan's expectations from the partnership were about having fun together, whereas John wants closeness as well.

It is not that one is right and the other is wrong, but that each lives in a somewhat different world, with disparate expectations, and they do not realize this. The grids do not provide the answers. They ask the questions.

What such exercises do is open up a dialogue, help establish key issues and produce an opportunity to work things through. Each person knows himself and his partner a little better, as well as what each expects out of the relationship. There are usually some surprises. The outcome can be the re-establishment of the partnership on a more realistic basis or a parting of the ways. This is preferable to being tied to a lifestyle that is emotionally poisonous.

Intimate partnerships, when they are satisfactory, not only provide a source of support, fun, sharing and companionship but also help to reduce stress. Being able to talk over your workday problems with a sympathetic partner helps reduce the negative effects of stress. If communication between the two of you becomes impossible, then not only do the negative effects remain – they are intensified. Sleep becomes disturbed and the next day you feel worn out before you even reach the office. Your partner then becomes an additional problem. To cope, you distance yourself from him or her and so help to destroy the relationship even more.

References

J. R. Adams-Weber, *Personal Construct Theory: Concepts and Applications* (Wiley, 1979.)

D. Bannister and F. Fransella, *Inquiring Man* (Penguin, 1971.)

N. Beail, *Repertory Grid Techniques and Personal Construct Psychology* (Croom Helm, 1985.)

F. Fransella and D. Bannister, *A Manual for Repertory Grid Techniques*, (Academic Press, 1977.)

G. Kelly, *The Psychology of Personal Constructs*, vols 1 and 2, (Norton, 1955.)

K. A. Powell, *Stress in Your Life* (Thorsons, 1988.)

——, *Repertory Grid Technique Workbook* (KAPA, 1990.)

6

FINDING AND GETTING
WHAT YOU WANT

EXPLORING NEW CAREER PATHS

Once you have started to get some control over circumstances that contribute to your burnout and have looked at some of the deeper issues discussed in Chapter 5, you should have begun to know yourself better. Some of the pressures should have been reduced. There should be some light at the end of the tunnel and you should feel some sense of hope. If a major part of your problem was connected with the sort of work you are (or were) doing, and you feel that you should move to another job, you need to spend some time examining how to do this.

You spend much of your life at work. What you do in your job has a major influence on how you feel, and can create tensions within your family.

Work can be much more than just a way of earning an income. Of course you want money, but you also need to enjoy what you do, feel you are working in a positive environment and with people to whom you can relate.

The aim of this chapter is to help you explore what you'd like to do with your working life.

If you have decided that you are in the right profession but the wrong organization, your plan will be to remove yourself from your present employers while remaining in the same profession. If you feel that what you are doing is somehow not right for you, you can use this chapter to examine the main issues connected with your choice of career.

You need time and some structured methods to weigh up whether to leave your present type of work and how and where to direct your energies. You need to think of immediate needs and also long-term goals. You may also need to consider other members of your family. You may have economic commitments that bind you to your present job for the time being.

CAREER CONSTRUCTS

Before you start with a more structured way of looking at what you want, try some work with visualization.

Day-dream about your ideal fantasy job. Let go of reality, just let your mind idle and observe what comes up. Imagine where you would be working, what you would be doing, what your fellow-workers would be like. What sort of lifestyle would you be living?

Compare what you do now with this fantasy. What is missing from your present life? Start to consider how some of the qualities that are missing could be achieved.

Now consider some major issues. Take a look at your personality; then your aptitudes; next, your preferences and interests and finally, how these might mesh with what is available in the job market. You may have to think of both long- and short-term action so that you move out of where you are into something less stressful while you prepare yourself for your long-term goals.

Your whole idea of what work means to you provides an important framework for beginning your considerations. Without this, you may be just tinkering with peripheral issues.

As a start, complete the following sentence, giving three

different answers:
 To me, work means . . .

1:
2:
3:

Close your eyes and let your imagination take over. Try to visualize what work means to you. Just let ideas and images drift into your mind. What emerges? Was it clear and bright? Dull and fuzzy? Nothing at all? Was there a theme? What did you feel? Nothing? A sense of foreboding? Excitement? Hostility? Dread?

 Your sentences may have looked something like this:

- . . . a way of earning a living.
- . . . something unpleasant I have to put up with.
- . . . an exciting, rewarding experience.
- . . . being exploited.
- . . . something that makes me tired and irritable on a Monday morning.
- . . . an important means of self-fulfilment.
- . . . being someone worthwhile.
- . . . something I have to do while waiting for my annual holiday.

All these comments have been made by individuals as they grappled with what they wanted out of a job.

 When you closed your eyes, you may have seen some kind of conflict in your mind's eye, a mass of work being imposed on you, some exciting scene, or a dull office on a wet, wintry Monday morning.

 Stay with your images. Ask yourself what they mean to you. Listen to yourself talking about work. You may find that a hidden part of you is expressing itself at last and that the ideas seem strange to you. Don't dismiss them. Remember, they are your ideas.

What emerges provides a clue about your work *meta-theme*.

Consider some of the examples mentioned earlier – for example: 'To me, work means a way of earning a living.' This suggests that work is just a means to an end. It doesn't have much other importance. The second example: '. . . something unpleasant I have to put up with', shows that work gets in the way of your real life. It does not add any pleasure to it. The third example: '. . . an exciting, rewarding experience', indicates that work is an important factor in your life.

Take a look at what you have written. As you did in the construct exercises in Chapter 5, also write down the opposites of your comments. Stay with what comes into your mind rather than working things out intellectually. Here are some examples – but do remember that your responses may be quite different:

- a way of earning a living<->a means of fulfilling myself.
- something unpleasant I have to put up with<-> something I enjoy doing most days.
- something painful<->an exciting, rewarding experience
- being exploited<->a co-operative enterprise.
- something that makes me tired and irritable on a Monday morning<->enjoying seeing my work colleagues once again.
- drudgery<->self-fulfilment
- not being myself<->being someone worthwhile.
- something I have to do while waiting for my annual holiday<->something that gives meaning to my life.

You can see from these statements that work itself can mean quite different things to different people. You need to examine the personal meaning you give your work. Face up to the inner reality of what you want. For this exercise, cut out the 'shoulds' and 'oughts'. You are taking a look at yourself. Maybe what you want is not feasible. But at least you should consider it. For you, work may be a mission in life or it may be something you'd rather not do at all.

C. Brooklyn Derr of the University of Utah, USA, has suggested that there are five orientations about work:

1: getting ahead
2: getting secure
3: getting free
4: getting high
5: getting balanced

Most of these are self-explanatory. Getting free is about personal autonomy. Getting high is concerned with excitement and action.

This was an American study and there are likely to be cultural differences depending on where in the world you are living and working. The economic development of a country fashions the framework in which ideas about employment exist.

Other research suggests that many of us work for no particular satisfaction but because it is a means of earning money. Taking Derr's work and those of others, seven major themes seem to emerge:

1. Career
   Here success is important; the goal is to strive for higher positions within an organization or profession.
2. Instrumental
   A way of earning a living that provides the material means to make life satisfactory – the life-blood of consumerism.
3. Security
   A way of meeting basic needs that enable you to exist. This

is likely to be the prime motivation in underdeveloped countries, where the struggle is just to stay alive. But it also applies elsewhere, where the world is perceived as unsafe and all efforts must be made to make things safer. The problem is that much of this insecurity is within the person, and however hard he or she tries to make the external world more certain, it doesn't affect his or her inner world.

4. Vocation

This is about using work to express your talents and aptitudes.

5. Doing your own thing

A way of self-development and growth. You expose yourself to different experiences in order to enhance who you are. This was very much a 'sixties' phenomenon.

6. Balance

An attempt to balance one aspect of life (work) with other aspects – such as personal relationships, politics, church, etc.

7. Taking what comes

Accepting what's available, either as a positive choice or because you feel that is how it should be. Many people are not over-concerned with money and the concept of a career is not in their consciousness.

These dimensions of work are not necessarily exclusive; for example, career might be combined with vocation. But there will be times when a choice has to be made – take promotion and sacrifice present satisfactions. Each dimension, within and between, can sow the seeds of stress and burnout. Matters can also be more subtle: you may feel that you 'should' pursue a career but inwardly you rebel. You may even have been 'processed' into a particular occupation by your parents. You remain because of the power they have over you (or you allow them to have over you) but inwardly you rebel.

You may have dedicated yourself to a vocation, but pressures from family or friends intrude. You may try to downgrade work to seek a more balanced life with your children and your hobbies, but your firm pressurizes you to return to your former commitment. Another problem may be that your partner does not share your attitude to work. Priorities differ. You operate in dissimilar worlds. Anger may cause clashes over the real issue or be displaced onto other, less relevant ones. You may argue about other matters but the energy for the conflict comes from the fundamental differences held by you both.

Let's look at each work dimension in more detail. All these orientations toward work have their advantages – but they also impose liabilities. By bringing such issues into the open, you become clearer about what you want. You may also see where much of your stress comes from and how your burnout has developed.

Career

This is about promotion. Status and financial rewards demand commitment and energy, and frequently require that you put other interests into second place – and this includes your family. You do not question (at least overtly) your company's assumptions – your viewpoint, tastes and leisure activities are fashioned by those who employ you; including even more subtle aspects, such as how you should look.

Fine – if this is what you really want, but playing a role that might deny other important parts of your personality has its costs. These can often include stress and, sometimes, burnout; because burnout becomes your only way out. You do not allow yourself to cut the strings – only something very dramatic can do that, like a breakdown or a heart attack. You may have heard people talk about their illness as the best thing that ever happened to them.

Sometimes we can get trapped into remaining in a career because we have acquired the commitments and lifestyle connected with that career and dismantling these would be costly in many ways.

As we get older, we begin to look over our shoulder and notice younger people eager to overtake us. If we have a 'Type A' personality, we have an inner need to be tough, thrusting and competitive. We 'need' the pressure, but it begins to take more and more out of us. We have to work harder to keep up.

Does this mean that career ambitions should be discarded? Not necessarily. Consider whether this is what you want. Take a look at its positive and negative aspects. You could even start to reconstrue the concept of a career and perhaps see it more as a game than a life compulsion. Note what pushes you over the top and learn to reduce or – better still – avoid such activities. If you feel that your career is not for you, then plan to move out. It will mean sacrifice. It will be difficult. But this is better than battling on in something which is getting increasingly distasteful.

Even if you enjoy your career, there can come a time when you feel you are getting nowhere. If you are very bright and specialized this can be a particular problem. You can become trapped in your expertise. What was once challenging is now boring. Your skills match your current work. Your salary is too high for you to retrain and start anew. Upward promotion is not possible. Scope to modify your present work is limited. Success has trapped you.

A Canadian study showed that people locked in in this way are usually older, have served longer, are more passive, conservative, dependent and less skilled at handling human relations problems. They feel dissatisfied, stressed and suffer from physical illnesses. These factors may result from, or be the cause of, their problems.

The remedy is prevention: don't let it happen. Review your

career from time to time.

In your imagination, work out a number of possible scenarios about where your work path is likely to lead. Capture how you might feel if some of these came true. If you don't like what emerges, take active steps to invest in a more positive future.

Discuss your problems with someone sympathetic. Examine how much of your worth as a person is bound up with being a success at work. The solution may lie in rebalancing your life so that other needs are met.

You may need conflicting satisfactions. The researcher Alderfer, in the US, suggests from empirical evidence that we have three major motivational needs:

1. existence
2. relatedness
3. growth

Our needs might operate at two or three levels at the same time, each with varying intensities. If we fail on one dimension we continue to persist. We also regress by putting more energy into other, less crucial needs. If career growth fails us, we still try, but put more energy into socializing and making new friends. Needs can be chronic – persisting over a long time – or temporary – altering as we get older or as circumstances change.

An interesting parallel idea is Erik Erikson's concept of life stages. Each has a crisis and negative or positive outcomes. Some of the stages are in childhood: in the first few months of life we acquire basic trust or mistrust. This lays the foundation for the way we trust or mistrust others during our lives. If we trust, we take risks when forming relationships. We become close or we cut ourselves off from intimate relationships.

The next stage builds on trust and offers us the choice of

autonomy or shame. Then follows initiative vs. guilt –
where if successful we assert ourselves and learn to act on our
environment and channel our energies usefully.

Next comes industry vs. inferiority. Either we learn to
become more competent or we see ourselves as failures.

The next move is connected with identity vs. role
confusion. We learn who we are. In some cultures this stage
is ritualized. Ceremonies transform us from child into adult.
In Western culture the transition is not clear-cut and we can
experience doubt and confusion. We may try out different
identities – being a rebel. With success emerges a strong self-
concept. Alternatively we remain confused about who we
are.

The next dilemma is about intimacy vs. isolation. Having
'found' our real selves, we now try to find another with
whom we can share our lives. To fail is to experience
isolation.

The next stage is called generativity vs. stagnation. We need
to be productive and creative. Mid-career crises may be
connected with this area. We can sense our stagnation. We
feel we are no longer getting anywhere. Whatever we do is
futile.

The final crisis is integrity vs. despair. As we approach the
end of our lives we will sum it all up and feel it has either
been worthwhile or that we have missed the boat and do not
have any more time or another life to try again.

These ideas provide a perspective for us to locate ourselves
in our life journey. They should only be used as suggestions
to help you question your life. They are not necessarily
binding for all people and all cultures.

Your route may be different. The stages may not be so clear
and distinct as Erikson suggests, but they provide guideposts
for immediate issues.

Instrumental

The second attitude to work is to see it as an instrument to obtain other things. What is important is money. Purchases define who you are. Your job may be boring but the pay packet at the end of the week or month is what it is all about. Your interests are your home, your hobbies, holidays, social activities and especially your possessions. You judge others by what they own.

Apart from an unfulfilling job, the prospects of change and redundancy threaten you because you feel that your value as a person is bound up with what you own and are able to buy. If such a crisis presents itself, it can be constructive because it might force you to review who you are and what you want out of work.

Security

You aim to play it safe. But today's uncertain world presents little safety. Civil service, banking, local government, law and accountancy, all previously 'safe' professions, are no longer so. Previously, loyalty was paid in return for security. We are hurt when we realize that this no longer applies.

The key is to realize that the only real security is within yourself and to develop competencies and skills that are marketable. It also helps to be flexible.

Vocation

Perhaps the greatest source of stress is connected with those of us who see work as a vocation. Then our jobs are central to living and our commitment makes it difficult to cut ourselves off from work. Everything is subordinated to our vocation. As discussed, idealism of this nature can turn into disillusionment.

Doing Your Own Thing

This may seem ideal, but it can still be a source of stress. Personal development is the motive. You are not concerned with moving upwards but with personal autonomy. Independence and control are important.

This aspect may involve changes which others puzzle over as they have no insight into your motivation. They may experience you as superficial because (to them) you exist on the margin of things. You are in the company or organization but not of it. You are an outsider (and you are glad that this is so). Your need for personal space creates distance between yourself and others. There are pressures for you to fit in with expectations; parents, partners and teachers remind you of the importance of a career and not just 'playing around' with life. The message is strong: settle down, and it can be stressful if you are not strong enough to remain secure in the knowledge that you have chosen the right path for yourself.

Balance

You may think the perfect answer is to strive for balance, to reconcile job demands with those of home and family. Superficially, you could allocate so many hours to work, to each of your children and of course to yourself. Trying to be fair, however, somehow doesn't seem to work. Family members clash over when they need you most.

Trying to achieve balance at a deeper level, where you attempt to impose some meaningful priorities on how you allocate your time, seems the answer. But the demands come at the wrong time: your daughter needs help with her examination preparation; your partner is facing a crisis; work demands some urgent action and your son wants to be left alone – but you sense he needs some special kind of help. You end up with a compromise and wonder where you went wrong. This can all be very stressful.

Taking What Comes

This is not an option most people would admit to. The problem is that letting things take their course may turn out to mean that you get something you dislike – at least some of the time.

DECIDING ON A CAREER

At a more detailed level, there are six areas to be explored about deciding what job to choose, if you are thinking of changing your profession. You need to consider:

1. your personality traits
2. your aptitudes and abilities
3. your training, qualifications and experience
4. your own interests
5. what is available
6. the practicalities of searching and applying for jobs

All these considerations need to fit together. If your mix of aptitudes points in a particular direction but you haven't the personality traits necessary for a particular line of work, you will find the job dissatisfying in some ways.

The best way to assess your personality is to take a personality test. Although these are far from perfect, they do provide a reasonably realistic idea of what sort of person you are. Of course, you need not be stuck with all aspects of your personality, but such tests give you an idea of where to start should you wish to alter your personality in some way.

Research confirms five major personality dimensions:

1. Extroverted/introverted
2. Toughminded/sensitive

3. Anxious/confident
4. Independent/dependent
5. Conscientious/expedient

No aspect is necessarily better than the others. Anxiety can produce drive, confidence apathy. Conscientiousness is obviously valuable – but so, at times, is expediency. Sometimes, what is necessary is balance. At other times, a limited degree rather than an extreme of a personality trait is needed – it depends on the demands of the job.

Here is a brief description of each trait. Most people (about 40 per cent) are in the middle, that is, slightly introverted or extroverted, not especially tough nor tenderminded, and so on.

Extroverted/Introverted

Extroverts are people who get their energy from others. They need to seek out other people and interact with them. They tend to be warm, friendly, outgoing, somewhat bold, enthusiastic, impulsive, energetic and openly emotional. They prefer risk-taking to playing it safe. Introverts get their energy internally; they are more cautious than extroverts, less excitable and prefer to think things through before acting; they like a clear-cut business organization, where all employees know where they stand and what their responsibilities are.

Toughminded/Sensitive

Toughminded persons are performance-orientated, they think in terms of results rather than for the feelings of others. Sensitive people are concerned with the feelings of others, they listen to what others have to say, they like to consult with others, and believe in participation rather than authoritarianism; they are empathetic and understanding.

Anxious/Confident

People who are anxious tend to feel insecure; they doubt their abilities, they never feel quite certain that they have taken the right decision, they worry – frequently over minor matters – they tend to be somewhat pessimistic. They can be upset by criticism, and are more emotional than those with more self-confidence. They may have an inner drive which aims at trying to make (from their perception) an uncertain world more certain. Within limits, all these traits can make positive contributions to an organization. There is value in doubt, an inner drive does get things done, and there is some evidence that pessimistic people are more realistic. Confident people are more self-assured and assertive, they are optimistic and can cope when the pressure is high, they enjoy the unexpected – all useful qualities, but too much confidence leads to unnecessary risk-taking.

Independent/Dependent

Independent persons prefer to take their own decisions and do things their own way. They tend to be unconventional. They are creative and flexible but are difficult to get along with. They certainly do not suit a highly structured, bureaucratic institution. Dependent people are more conservative, preferring clear guidelines and procedures. They are usually more practical and down-to-earth. They prefer to make decisions with others rather than on their own. They are not risk-takers.

Conscientious/Expedient

Conscientious people are self-disciplined, consistent, persevering, can be relied on, are tidy, follow rules and do not cut corners. They are practical people, but are more rule-bound than their expedient counterparts. Expedient persons are more unconventional and impulsive, are easily frustrated by rules, and will cut corners to get things done.

You may have noticed that there is some overlap within some of these traits; for example: expedient people tend to be impulsive – so do extroverts. This means that someone who is both an extrovert *and* expedient is more likely to be impulsive than one who has just one of these traits. Some traits counterbalance others.

Now that you have some idea of what the traits mean, you can begin to assess your personality. Take a look at the example below. Place a cross at any point between the two extremes of personality, depending upon how much of each trait you possess. Of course, this is not as accurate as a full personality test, but it will provide you with some ideas about yourself.

Example:

Extroverted	x	Introverted
Toughminded	x	Sensitive
Anxious	x	Confident
Independent	x	Dependent
Conscientious	x	Expedient

By joining the points together, you get a profile. The example above shows a somewhat introverted, sensitive, rather anxious, dependent, fairly conscientious person who will want to play safe, needs a clearly structured organization with clear rules and procedures, and who will want others to make decisions for him but can be relied on to carry out what he is told to do. He won't take risks and he is likely to spend much of his time worrying about whether he has got things right.

Now try your profile:

Extroverted		Introverted
Toughminded		Sensitive
Anxious		Confident
Independent		Dependent
Conscientious		Expedient

You might like to get a friend, work colleague or your partner to do a profile about you (but don't show them the one you've already done on yourself). Compare how others see you with the way you assess yourself. If results are similar, you've probably got it right. If not, consider how you would amend the profile.

Now think of what sort of profile would suit the jobs or career you are considering.

As it is likely that a range within each personality dimension would suit, place two crosses to assess this range for each of the traits, for example:

Personality Profile needed for a particular job:

Extroverted	x x		Introverted
Toughminded	x x		Sensitive
Anxious		x x	Confident
Independent	x x		Dependent
Conscientious		x x	Expedient

This example shows that this job (let's say a department manager) requires a reasonably extroverted person who is toughminded, not too anxious, quite independent and really expedient. But a person with these qualities taken to extremes – someone highly extroverted, very toughminded, totally independent and completely expedient – would not do!

Draw up a profile of the job you want to go for. Now compare it with your personality profile. How well do you suit the job? You can do this for any number of different jobs you might be considering.

Remember, you are not completely stuck with your personality as it is now. Within reason you can work to improve things. For example, you could try to reduce your levels of anxiety, you could learn to become more independent – and so on.

Many jobs require a mixture of aptitudes. Although an aptitude test is needed to assess these correctly, you can gain some idea by looking at what subjects you were good at in school and college, and at which ones appeal to you. There are many different types of aptitudes, but the main ones are:

- verbal
- numerical
- perceptual

Verbal aptitude is the capacity to see relationships in terms of words; numerical aptitude: in terms of figures, and perceptual aptitude: through shapes, diagrams and graphics.

There are two important aspects to be considered: how much of each aptitude you possess and the differentials between a set of aptitudes, which go towards making up an overall profile. High verbal and low perceptual points to a basic 'arts' orientation away from quantitative analyses (and away from the graphic arts) and into such areas as law, teaching, or journalism. The opposite profile, with perceptual the highest and verbal the lowest is a 'science' profile, where direct observation and the analysis of such observation is important. Where numerical aptitude predominates, accountancy or commercial areas are suggested (provided there is a reasonably high quantity of each of the other two aptitudes).

Social workers, teachers and nurses often have high verbal and high perceptual aptitudes, more or less in balance. A flat profile, where all dimensions are equal, indicates an 'all-rounder', the person not able to focus in any particular direction.

Now assess your aptitudes:

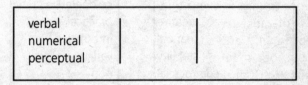

Again, within limits, you can improve your abilities in each of these directions, or you may choose to develop the strengths you already possess even further.

Your next area to consider is your training, qualifications and experience.

First list your academic qualifications, then your specialist training, followed by all the courses you have taken, and then your work experience.

Now think of jobs that you might be interested in and list what qualifications and experience might be required. Compare this list with your own qualifications and experience profile. You may find a good match, or you may need to take additional qualifications. If you are not certain what you need to do, local colleges will often help. Ring them up and ask for an informal chat.

Of special importance is your own interests. These are things you would like to do in your job.

The best way to find out your preferences is to take what is called an 'interest bank' test, but you can get some idea by working through the following exercise.

Preference Profile:

Organization:	large	small
Travel:	little	extensive
Indoors:	mostly	outdoors
Security:	high	risk
Independence:	high	low
People:	working with	alone
	competitive	co-operative
	creative	practical
	manual	intellectual
	stability	variety
	commercial	non-commercial
	pressurized	calm
	computational	not figure work

It can be useful to put your profile chart away for a week or two and prepare another one, without referring to the first. Compare the two. If there are differences, this might reflect your changing mood at the times you wrote out the two profiles.

Draw a profile of where potential jobs are likely to fit into this chart and compare how they fit in with your own preferences.

The next stage is to look more deeply at how you construe different jobs.

To do so you need to work through a repertory grid similar to the one outlined in Chapter 5, except this time concentrate on work, not stress.

First of all, go through the job vacancies in the newspapers. Mark all those jobs you'd like to do (even if you feel you are unqualified for them). Also mark those you would definitely *not* like to do. Ignore other jobs which you are uncertain about or which you do not particularly like or dislike. Go through the ones you've marked again and highlight those that especially appeal to you.

Go through those you dislike and add another mark against those you particularly dislike.

A pattern should emerge that suggests which type of work you think you would enjoy and which you would find distasteful.

The elements to help you construct your grid are:

1. A job you would really like doing; not taken from the newspaper
2. A job you would dislike doing (not necessarily from the newspaper)
3. A job you have selected as especially positive from your look through the papers (not one already mentioned above)
4. Another positive job from the newspaper survey
5. A job selected from your newspaper survey that you would especially dislike
6. Another positive one
7. Your present job (or the last one you had)

Now take the first three elements:

1. A job you would really like doing
2. A job you would dislike doing
3. A job you have selected as especially positive from the newspaper (not one already mentioned above)

Ask yourself what qualities 1 and 3 share. You may find this straightforward or rather difficult. You may have a vague feeling about what it is that the two share which is difficult to put into words. If it is difficult to verbalize, try to imagine the feeling as a shape or symbol or let it form a scene. What word or words come into your mind connected with it? Of course, it is also quite likely that a clear-cut phrase will come into your mind.

Note down a word or phrase which captures the quality that points 1 and 3 share.

You may have written something like this (but do stay with your own ideas, even if they are quite different):

- status
- fulfilment
- a pleasant way of earning a living

Now think of the opposite. Make sure this feels right for you, even if it isn't the strict dictionary definition of this concept's opposite.

For the above examples, you might write:

- status<->being nobody
- fulfilment<->wasting my life
- a pleasant way of earning a living<->an unpleasant way

Now look again at 1 and 3 – are there any other qualities that they share? Note these and their opposites. Then look at number 1 alone. Are there any additional qualities that you have not already noted? Add them to your list, along with their opposites. Repeat the exercise with number 3. Then look at number 2, where the opposite will be the positive quality.

What you have done is to elicit constructs connected with work in your life.

Here is an example and then a grid form for your personal use. Place the negative pole of each construct on the left-hand side of the construct space. This will make it easier for you later on.

Figure 16: Sample Work Grid

constructs	1 Journalist	2 Accountant	3 Public Relations Officer	4 Recruitment Consultant	5 Fundraiser	6 Scriptwriter	7 Marketing	8 Ideal	9	10	11
1 routine – creative	4	2	4	3	3	5	3	4			
2 task-orientated – people-orientated	4	1	4	4	3	3	3	4			
3 passive – plenty of activity	5	1	4	4	4	3	3	4			
4 static – dealing with new things	5	2	4	4	4	3	4	5			
5 manager – specialist	5	5	5	4	5	5	4	4			
6 mechanistic – organic	5	1	4	3	4	4	4	4			
7 tedious – exciting	4	1	4	4	2	4	4	4			
8 stagnant – self-developing	4	1	3	2	4	4	4	4			
9 poorly paid – well paid	3	5	4	4	3	4	3	3			

elements

constructs

Figure 17: Work Grid for You to Use

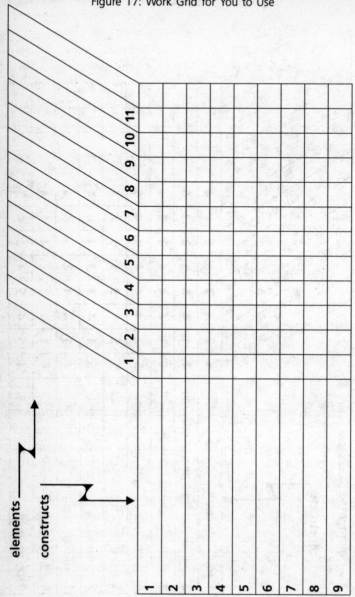

You can see that along the top are the elements and along the side the constructs, with the negative pole on the left-hand side and the more positive one on the right.

You now need to repeat the exercise with different combinations from your list of jobs you would and would not like:

4, 5 and 6

1, 4 and 7

2, 4 and 5

3, 6 and 7

Some of the combinations are not straightforward – two positive and one negative. This is intentional, to enable you to elicit many constructs. Remember to place the more positive pole on the right and the negative one on the left.

What you need to do now is to rate each construct against each element on a scale of 1 to 5, placing this 'score' in the box opposite the construct and under the element. Give a rating of 1 if the left-hand (negative) pole of the construct fully applies, 5 if it does not apply, and 2, 3 or 4 for anything in between. A rating of 3, for example, would be given if the construct does not apply or if both poles are equally balanced. Note how these boxes are filled in as shown in Figure 16.

As you saw in the Chapter 5, which introduced repertory grids, you can get an idea of more important constructs by seeing how the rows link together. Similarities suggest relationship constructs. Compare each row with every other row. Similarities mean that there are just one or two differences in a few of the ratings.

There are also statistical techniques that use computers to work out the relationships for you (cluster, principal component analysis, factor analysis, elementary linkage analysis, etc.). If you can get your grid analysed in this way, you may find it provides useful insights into how you perceive your world of work.

Now you need to add another element, as shown in Figure 16. This goes in column 8 above, and is your 'Ideal' job. Rate this.

Look at the figures given for your present or last job and your 'ideal job'. How do they differ?

You can measure how your present job differs from the ideal one by comparing the ratings for your current job and your ideal job (element 8) for each construct. Figure out the difference between the two scores. A more powerful way is to calculate a correlation between the two. Less than +.3 indicates a fair degree of job dissatisfaction.

The grid will show where your dissatisfactions lie, the intensity of each dissatisfaction, and gives you a list of qualities that are important to you in a job.

You can add further columns for jobs you are thinking of applying for, rating them as you think they would apply to each construct and then comparing them with your present (or last) job and your ideal job.

To help you make a decision, you have to decide how important each construct is to you. Some will be more important than others.

With all these exercises, note which themes emerge. Look at inconsistencies. If you feel uncomfortable with some issues, don't push doubts away, face them. Maybe part of what you're telling yourself to do is based on old parental messages in your head about how you should live your life. Examine these, trace them back in your life. Your parents may not have actually spelled out an attitude to work to you but this is what it adds up to. For example:

Your father's message might have been: 'Push everything you've got into it.'

Your mother's might have been: 'You'll never make it however hard you try.'

You can see the inconsistency. It is an impossible way to live, because it means that even if you put everything you've got into work, you'll never really make it. So you'll keep on trying even harder. Were their messages positive, destructive or just unhelpful? The key point is that you need not remain bound to them.

When you have worked through these exercises and come to some tentative conclusions, your next step is to check what's available in your areas of interest in the job market. You may also have to consider a job's location. Family or other commitments may limit your choice.

All these exercises do not form a straight, linear progression. They are more like a spiral: you get some tentative ideas, explore further, modify early ideas, test things out and repeat the process, further refining your ideas each time. What you have done is to start moving, and once you've started, you can always change direction. You may find that your constructs change, that you feel like giving some of them different ratings or that your priorities vary. This is fine. But there will come a time when you need to make concrete plans and start to put them into action.

You will have to make choices and perhaps compromises. You may have to postpone doing what you really want to do until you have acquired additional qualifications or until your personal commitments change.

Here is what some people who have worked through these exercises have decided:

'I am going to get a job in the country, preferably manual work, and live on a house boat.'

'I am going to get a qualification to teach English as a foreign language in an Eastern European country.'

'I am going to take half pension now and get a job three days a week as an accountant with a charity.'

'I am going to move to a Scottish island and take any nursing job that is available.'

'I am going to move out of the city and get a teaching job in a smaller community.'

'I want to write. I am going to move to the country and run a small guest house to help with finances.'

'I am going to buy a mobile food van and sell good-quality meals in country areas.'

'I am going to give up teaching and become a librarian.'

'I am going to start a theme shop in a small town, build up from there and run others as a franchise.'

'I want to give up being a doctor and become a lawyer.'

Your next task is to find out what is available. You will already have some information from examining the newspapers.

How you can explore this further depends upon what you are looking for. Here are some starting points:

1. Ask colleagues and friends
2. Write to potential employers
3. Prepare a proposal and contact sponsors
4. Newspapers
5. Professional journals
6. Colleges and other institutes
7. Professional societies
8. Recruitment agencies
9. Executive search agencies
10. Local career service
11. Employment centres
12. Small Firms Service
13. Chambers of Commerce
14. Directories
15. Advertising for what you want

For example, you could visit a town in which you'd like to live and call in at employment agencies, look through local directories for suitable employers, visit the local careers advisory service, search through recent issues of the local press, or call in at the local Chamber of Commerce.

All this takes time and needs persistence. You may find that you have set your sights too high and need to lower them. You may feel some avenues are blocked and that you have to try a different approach. Conversely, you may find that you are offered more than one suitable job and are not too certain which to take!

You can also consider a portfolio of different employment possibilities, perhaps having a rather dull part-time job to provide a basic income and then one or two other jobs which are more fulfilling. You could also consider a co-operative arrangement, whereby a number of like-minded people work together, sharing facilities and providing a support network.

Do not try just one thing at a time, fire a number of shots simultaneously. Have a number of fall-back plans rather than an 'all or nothing' approach. Allow yourself to be imaginative in your job search. Do things which are out of the ordinary, rather than just what everyone else does.

Have a CV or resumé prepared. If you have access to a word processor, you can easily modify your standard CV to suit the organizations to which you are applying. If you have a desk-top publishing package, so much the better. You can give your CV a professional touch.

Make your CV brief. List your academic qualifications, experience, age and personal details. Add something that helps you stand out from the crowd. Enclose a short covering letter in which you state why you feel you are suitable for the post.

Before you go for an interview, look up as much as you can about the business. List what you think they are looking for and why you feel that you are especially suitable. Make a note of important questions you want to ask, because you need to find out as much as possible about how suitable the job is for you.

Your interview is likely to start with open and general questions and then become more detailed. If you are unclear about what you are being asked, define the question in your terms and check with the interviewer that you have understood what is being asked. While you don't need to volunteer adverse information, you should reply honestly and openly.

If you don't succeed, review the interview. Did you fail because you did not meet the specifications of the job fully or because of poor interviewing techniques? If the latter – what needs to be improved? If you realize that you are unskilled and that your lack of effective interview techniques is letting you down, there are training courses on interviewing that could help. You can practise until you become proficient. If you really are very nervous, you could try relaxation exercises (see the ones mentioned in Chapter 4), or get some professional help in gaining more confidence. But, remember that some degree of 'nerves' is normal and can actually be helpful.

These exercises take time; you may have to 'kick-start' yourself initially to get going. But you will have started on the path to a more fulfilling work life. *Good luck!*

References

C. P. Alderfer, *Existence, Relatedness and Growth: Human Needs in an Organizational Setting* (Free Press, 1972.)

R. C. Cattell, *The Scientific Analysis of Personality* (Pelican, 1965.)

C. Brooklyn Derr, 'Career switching and organization policies', in Katz (ed.), *Career Issues in Human Resource Management* (Prentice-Hall, 1982.)

——, *Career Policies: Theories and Methods for Career Success* (Institute of Human Resource Management, 1982.)

E. Erikson, *Childhood and Society* (Paladin, 1978.)

A. D. Kantel, *Work and Family in the US* (Sage, 1977.)

H. L. Willensky, 'Work, careers and social integration', *International Journal of Social Sciences*, 12.243, 1960.

AFTERWORD

Most people do not read non-fiction books from cover to cover. You have probably selected to read the parts of this book that could be most helpful to you in your particular situation. You will also have noticed that, although your problems are unique to you, many of the stories reported by fellow burnout sufferers have reflected your own dilemma. Remember, all of them found a way out of burnout – and so can you.

Your first priority is to reduce the heat so that you can review where you are. If you feel you cannot change the main cause of your stress, you need to plan to remove yourself from it. This is a tough but important decision, and one you need to accept as soon as possible.

Your experiences, no matter how bad, can be seen to have some value if you examine the meaning behind your stressors and can begin to reconstruct yourself and your world. It is also helpful is to learn to relax so that the effects of your daily hassles and strains are diminished.

By taking the advice in this book which you feel is of help to you and putting it into practice, you will gain a vital edge: control. Feeling that you are actually in control is liberating. You no longer feel imprisoned but can make choices about life. You begin to see opportunities where previously there seemed to be none.

Start from where you are. Take small steps. Results will not be immediate, but they will come if you persevere. You do not have to remain a victim of burnout.

USEFUL ADDRESSES

UK

British Association for Counselling
1 Regent Place
Rugby, Warwicks CV21 2PJ
(For details of counselling services in the UK)

Dr M. Heap
British Society for Experimental & Clinical Hypnosis
Department of Psychology
Middleswood Hospital
Sheffield S6 1TP
(For details of qualified doctors, dentists, psychologists and
hypnotherapists in the UK)

Centre for Stress Management
156 Westcombe Hill
Blackheath, London SE3 7HP
(For training in stress management)

KAPA Consultancy
PO Box 222
Cheltenham GL51 5YL

(For in-company stress reduction workshops, individual counselling, grid analyses and relaxation cassettes)

USA

American Psychological Association
1200 Seventeenth Street NW
Washington, D. C. 20036

AUSTRALIA

Australian Society for Clinical & Experimental Hypnosis
Royal Melbourne Hospital
Royal Parade
Parkville
Victoria

NEW ZEALAND

New Zealand Psychological Society
Department of Education
University of Auckland
Private Bag
Auckland

SOUTH AFRICA

South Africa Psychological Association
PO Box 4292
Johannesburg

INDEX